# Build On The Rock

*366 Short Thoughts For Building Your Life On Christ*

**by H. Lamar Smith**

**Build On The Rock**
*366 Short Thoughts For Building Your Life On Christ*
Copyright © 2019 by H. Lamar Smith
Published as a Kindle book in 2019
Published as a paperback book in 2019

**Other Books by H. Lamar Smith**

In Paperback and Kindle

***In The Steps of The Shepherd***
*366 Short Thoughts for the Long Walk*

***The Disciples and The Teacher***
*366 Short Thoughts for Serious Disciples*

***Staying On The Way***
*366 Short Thoughts for 'Walking The Jesus' Way*

***Springs In Dry Places***
*366 Short Thoughts For Thirsty Souls*

***Captives Of Love***
*366 Short Thoughts For Christ's Bond Servants*

***The Master's Table***
*366 Short Thoughts For Hungry Disciples*

***Seasons for Deepening The Soul***
Kindle Only
*134 Short Devotional Readings for your walk through Lent, Holy Week, the Seasons of Easter, and Seasons of Pentecost. There are 118 days outlined with 134 readings.*

# Permissions

Scripture quotations marked (NASB) are from the New American Standard Bible®, Copyright © 1960, 1962, 1963, 1968, 1971, 1972, 1973, 1975, 1977, 1995 by The Lockman Foundation Used by permission." (www.Lockman.org)

Scripture quotations marked (NIV) are from THE HOLY BIBLE, NEW INTERNATIONAL VERSION®, NIV® Copyright © 1973, 1978, 1984, 2011 by Biblica, Inc.™ Used by permission. All rights reserved worldwide.

Scripture quotations marked (ESV) are from the ESV® Bible (The Holy Bible, English Standard Version®), copyright © 2001 by Crossway, a publishing ministry of Good News Publishers. Used by permission. All rights reserved.

Scripture quotations marked (NRSV) are from the New Revised Standard Version Bible, copyright © 1989 National Council of the Churches of Christ in the United States of America. Used by permission. All rights reserved.

Scripture quotations marked (NKJV) are from the New King James Version®. Copyright © 1982 by Thomas Nelson. Used by permission. All rights reserved.

Scripture quotations marked (The Message) are from THE MESSAGE. Copyright © by Eugene H. Peterson 1993, 1994, 1995, 1996, 2000, 2001, 2002. Used by permission of Tyndale House Publishers, Inc.

Scripture quotations marked (NLT) are taken from the *Holy Bible*, New Living Translation, copyright © 1996, 2004, 2015 by Tyndale House Foundation. Used by permission of Tyndale House Publishers, Inc., Carol Stream, Illinois 60188. All rights reserved.

Scripture quotations marked (KNT) are from The Kingdom New Testament: *A Contemporary Translation*. Copyright © 2011 by Nicholas Thomas Wright. HarperCollins Publishers. Used by permission. All rights reserved.

**Dedicated**

to

Dr. H. Ray Dunning

*Teacher, Mentor and Friend whose influence has been like yeast in my life.*

# Contents

| | |
|---|---|
| Title Page | page 1 |
| Books by Author | page 2 |
| Permissions | page 3 |
| Dedication | page 4 |
| Contents | page 5 |
| About the Author | page 6 |
| Recommendations | pages 7-9 |
| Foreword | page 10 |
| Note to Reader | page 11 |
| Introduction | page 12 |
| 366 Devotionals | pages 13-155 |
| Other Books | page 156 |

## About the Author

H. Lamar Smith has served as senior pastor for 46 years, having pastored in Tennessee, Kentucky, Oklahoma and Alabama.

Trevecca Nazarene University is his Alma Mater from which he received both the B.A. and M.A. degrees.

He has been a teacher of preachers, first in Nazarene Bible College Extension and later as teacher and Director of Alabama Nazarene School of Ministry. Many of his students have looked to him as mentor and confidant.

He also served as Executive Assistant to the District Superintendent on the Alabama North District Church of the Nazarene for five years.

He speaks in local churches for revivals, interim pulpit supply and Faith-Promise services. He speaks in workshops and in spiritual retreats for pastors.

He and his wife Danner love to camp as well as spend time with their families. Between them they have 11 grandchildren and 1 great-grand child.

He enjoys writing, building, gardening and fishing.

# Devotional Recommendations

"H. Lamar Smith's words come from a father's heart, written with a kindness learned from the backroads of personal pain. I find him always mindful of the reader's journey without placating or soft-soaping the truth. I am a student of his honed pen and honored to call him my friend."

Paulette B. Woods, Retired Pastor's Wife, Artist and Writer, Bethany, OK

\*\*\*


"The inspirational and sage wisdom of H. Lamar Smith serves as an encouragement and challenge to my walk with Jesus. His devotional thoughts are a welcomed part of my daily exercise. He has been called "a modern day Oswald Chambers"; you will come to recognize that and be inspired as you read through his anointed thoughts and revelations! Enjoy, and drink deep!"

Lynn Holmes, Lead Pastor Calvary Church
CEO of Calvary Pictures, (The Grace Card & INDIVISIBLE)
Memphis, TN

\*\*\*

"Lamar Smith's lifetime of ministry has given him a deep understanding of people and of the power of Scripture. His devotionals are pithy, witty and practical. They are like a protein bar for spiritual hunger, one bite-sized devotional delivers a lot of nourishment."

Robert Craft, Founder and Director of Reach A Village

\*\*\*

"Lamar is the most gifted writer I read. In a small space, he can pack truth and light that I need for my daily walk with God. He has the ability to speak to everyone that loves God and is seeking His will. Last Christmas we gave *In The Steps Of The Shepherd*, one of Lamar's devotional books, to tenants with a gift card at Christmas and have had several to thank me for the devotional book. I leave them in our house in Colorado and have had people to ask if they can take them. Thank you, Lamar, for answering God's call and continuing to do His work."

Phil Thrasher, Retired Teacher
Louisville, KY

\*\*\*

"I would like to express my deepest appreciation for the wonderful devotionals written by my friend, colleague and mentor, Lamar Smith. Lamar's writings are scholarly and theologically sound. They are a great way to start or end your day. Thank you, Lamar."

Pastor Joe McNulty, Cornerstone Church of the Nazarene, Cullman, AL

\*\*\*

"I appreciate Lamar Smith's writings and devotionals because he isn't afraid to deal with subject matter that has long been confusing or acting as stumbling blocks to many as they walk the Christian journey, such as: failures, maturing in one's faith, and misunderstandings about sanctification. These devotionals have provided much insight and depth for me. I have shared his books with many friends, and I will continue to look forward to new thoughts and helpful ways to begin my day. You have a gift and you are allowing God to use it to bless and inspire others. Thank you for your inspiration to others."

Peggy King, Retired Teacher and Army Chaplain's Wife
Dandridge, TN

\*\*\*

# Foreword

These devotional thoughts have come out of my own devotional life over the last several years. Many of these have been sent out as e-mails or included on social media sites. My devotional books are in direct response to many of my readers who have asked that these devotional thoughts be published in book form for regular and repeated readings. I send these forth with my heart's desire that they may be a blessing and a means of grace to my regular readers and new readers alike.

The devotionals contained here are written with the intention that they be short and to the point. It is my hope that they will be a spring-board of meaning throughout your day. You can read each of them in about a minute, but I trust that throughout your day they will be food for thought.

H. Lamar Smith

# Note To Reader

*Build On The Rock* is sent to you with the prayer that these short thoughts would be like mortar and a catalyst to attach us more and more to the Rock Jesus.

These 366 devotional thoughts can be used as a part of your daily devotionals or as touchstones for meditation. Feel free to share them with your friends.

You have permission to quote any of these individual devotional thoughts in social media or your other writings. When doing so you may use the following statement. "Quoted from *Build On The Rock* by H. Lamar Smith, Used by Permission."

Each reading has a month-date indication above the title for those who want to follow the Christian calendar in their readings. When the Christian calendar does not conform to the month-date numbering here, and most years it will not, you can begin reading 2-26 on Ash Wednesday and read through 6-7 then go back or forward to pick up the skipped readings.

You may subscribe for free daily devotional emails at: http://christourholyway.com

# Introduction

Jesus said, "Therefore everyone who hears these words of Mine and acts on them, may be compared to a wise man who built his house on the rock. "And the rain fell, and the floods came, and the winds blew and slammed against that house; and yet it did not fall, for it had been founded on the rock. Everyone who hears these words of Mine and does not act on them, will be like a foolish man who built his house on the sand. "The rain fell, and the floods came, and the winds blew and slammed against that house; and it fell—and great was its fall." Matthew 7:24-27 (NASB)

Jesus is life's foundation stone. He is the Rock on which you are to build your life. "For no man can lay a foundation other than the one which is laid, which is Jesus Christ" (I Corinthians 3:11). On Christ we can build reliably with Him as our Rock. Satan would have you build on unstable rubble and shifting sand. Examine yourself! Is Jesus really the foundation on which you are building your life? Are you acting on Jesus' teachings? Are His words important to you? Are they constantly transforming you? Rock or sand? The storm is coming!

May the thoughts that follow be a means of grace to you as you continue building your life on Christ the Rock.

# *Build On The Rock*

**1-1**
## Lean On The Rock
Sometimes the people that we think are solid rocks in our lives can crumble in their own human frailty. There is One on Whom you can lean in your life in the coming year. Build your life on Jesus and His words, and you will stand (Matthew 7:24). When you feel the ground you have stepped on begin to move, check your bearings and step back onto the Rock. Lean on Him. He can support all of your weight along with the burdens you carry. He cares; He invites you to build on the Rock.

"For You are my rock and my fortress; For Your name's sake You will lead me and guide me" Psalm 31:3 (NASB).

**1-2**
## Cornerstone
The builders select stones to fit into the wall. Certain sizes and shapes are selected for this or that spot. Sometimes a stone that looks as if it would never fit in the building, and has been cast aside, is the very stone needed, the cornerstone. God is building His temple on Jesus the Cornerstone. When our building is rightly related to Him as the essential Stone, then the house will stand.

"This Jesus is 'the stone that was rejected by you, the builders; it has become the cornerstone.' Acts 4:11 (NRSV)

**1-3**
## Keystone
An arch depends on a keystone. It is that special stone against which both sides of the arch push; it holds the whole arch in place. It is the stone on which the weight of the building above rests; in that regard, it is foundational. Jesus is the Keystone. Rest the whole structure on Him and it will stand. "The stone that the builders rejected has become the very head of the corner" (Acts 4:11). Make the keystone of the church to be program, personality or politics and it will fall. The temple centered in Christ and His indwelling Spirit will survive and thrive.

## 1-4
### Living Stones
We view stones as cold, solid, static and lifeless. Temples throughout the ages were built of this kind of stone. The early church had a vision of a new temple made up of living stones. Jesus was the living Cornerstone, proven by His resurrection from the dead. He had built around Himself disciples and followers who were made living stones by His Spirit. This is a dynamic temple, and organism vibrating with the very life of God. An inviting place. A warm place. A transforming place. A home for the soul. A spiritual house. A dwelling place for the very Spirit of God.

"And coming to Him as to a living stone which has been rejected by men, but is choice and precious in the sight of God, you also, as living stones, are being built up as a spiritual house for a holy priesthood, to offer up spiritual sacrifices acceptable to God through Jesus Christ." 1 Peter 2:4-5 (NASB)

## 1-5
### Built For Sacrifice
"You also, as living stones, are being built up as a spiritual house for a holy priesthood, to offer up spiritual sacrifices acceptable to God through Jesus Christ" (1 Peter 2:5 (NASB). We are a spiritual house. We are a holy priesthood serving in that house. Priests offer sacrifices. Jesus, the High Priest, offered up Himself. We, His disciples, are to offer up ourselves to God as living sacrifices (Romans 12:1-2). We offer our sacrifice in light of His sacrifice and through His sacrifice. In this mystery we are, as Paul said, "Co-crucified with Christ" (Galatians 2:20).

## 1-6
### A Welcoming House
Some houses are welcoming and inclusive to all; some shut others out as not worthy. God looked down and envisioned a hospitality house where strangers and aliens could come into the house as full-fledged family members. This is what the church is supposed to be. This is the kind of house where God will dwell. The unwelcoming house for the stranger cannot welcome the Lord either. In a welcoming church you will find God's Spirit dwelling there in full fellowship with the people. The other kind of church only offers fellowship with each other.

"So then you are no longer strangers and aliens, but you are citizens with the saints and also members of the household of God, built upon the foundation of the apostles and prophets, with Christ Jesus himself as the cornerstone. In him the whole structure is joined together and grows into a holy temple in the Lord; in whom you also are built together spiritually into a dwelling place for God." Ephesians 2:19-22 (NRSV)

## 1-7
### Stumbling Stone

A stone can serve as a step; it can also be a rock that trips you and makes you fall. We don't usually think of Jesus as someone who would make you stumble. Truth is, folks stumble over Him all the time. They stumble over His claims because they will not believe. Unbelief destines us to fall. Disobedience to Him trips us up. Trusting our life to Him enables us to stand. To those who stand, He is a Stone most precious.

"For it stands in scripture: 'See, I am laying in Zion a stone, a cornerstone chosen and precious; and whoever believes in him will not be put to shame.' To you then who believe, he is precious; but for those who do not believe, 'The stone that the builders rejected has become the very head of the corner,' and 'A stone that makes them stumble, and a rock that makes them fall.' They stumble because they disobey the word, as they were destined to do." 1 Peter 2:6-8 (NRSV)

## 1-8
### The New Sacrificial System

The line from the song, "Whiter Than Snow" prays, "Help me to make a complete sacrifice." Jesus put an end to offering animal sacrifices by the sacrifice of Himself. This, however, did not take sacrifice out of Christianity. The new sacrificial system is that we "Present our bodies a living sacrifice". To follow the Lamb is also to follow in sacrifice. Christianity without sacrifice is anemic and weak with no power to transform us or our world.

"Therefore I urge you, brethren, by the mercies of God, to present your bodies a living and holy sacrifice, acceptable to God, which is your spiritual service of worship. And do not be conformed to this world, but be transformed by the renewing of your mind, so that you may prove what the will of God is, that which is good and acceptable and perfect." Romans 12:1-2 (NASB)

## 1-9
### Precious To The Lord
As a pastor I have sat beside the bed of believers as they transitioned out of this life to be received into the Presence of the Lord. Some still stand out in my memory. It is sacred beyond solemnity. I often felt I was standing on holy ground. There was a sense that "the Lord is in this place". There is another side to it beyond the earthly side; there is God's perspective, the heavenly side. The One who notices the fall of a sparrow is always gloriously present with the passing of His children. It is precious to Him. "Precious in the sight of the LORD is the death of his saints" (Psalm 116:15 NIV). Oh, to live and die as one of His, and to hear Him say, "Well done" will make every mile, burden and pain disappear into glorious bliss.

## 1-10
### He Became The Sacrifice
Our God does not sacrifice humans or even animals for his own pleasure or appeasement. He sacrifices Himself on our behalf. Jesus, by His death, ended animal sacrifice forever when He became the "Lamb of God that takes away the sin of the world." He took upon Himself the results of a fallen creation, not by blaming them, not by destroying them, not by sacrificing them, but by becoming the sacrifice Himself. This is the revelation of God's heart toward sinners; this is a full demonstration of the love of God to all humankind. I fall down amazed!

"But when Christ came as a high priest of the good things that have come, then through the greater and perfect tent (not made with hands, that is, not of this creation), he entered once for all into the Holy Place, not with the blood of goats and calves, but with his own blood, thus obtaining eternal redemption." Hebrews 9:11-12 (NRSV)

## 1-11
### Ruling As In Following
We make a lot of the day when Christ will rule the nations; it will be a great day. We must not, however, forget that His rule has already begun, and further, we must not forget that Christ ruling the nations is far more than knees bowing before His throne. Jesus rules the nations when His ways are followed by the nations. His Kingdom comes every time His will is done on earth as in heaven; it

comes every time we follow His manner of living in the difficult places of our lives. That's what Him ruling and us bowing the knee looks like.

"And the seventh angel sounded; and there were great voices in heaven, saying, The kingdoms of this world are become the kingdoms of our Lord, and of his Christ; and he shall reign for ever and ever." Revelation 11:15 (KJV)

## 1-12
### More Than One Side
You have heard it said, "There are two sides to every story". There are sometimes dozens of sides. Like the facets of a diamond are all the factors that influence the disagreements and divisions among us. The factors that influence all sides are: cultural streams, one-sided talking points, blind loyalty, dysfunctional conditioning, injured souls, anger issues, agendas, pride, an inordinate need to be right, etc. The point of all of this is that thoughtful people need to see these threads in themselves as well as others. Using a principle from 1 Peter 3:7, we are to live with each other in "understanding ways so that our prayers are not hindered"; to say it in another way, our unthoughtful relationships with our fellow humans affect our relationship with the Father. Relationships are essential to good harmony, but we must know that it often takes tedious thought in how we should relate to each other.

## 1-13
### Pleasing What or Whom?
There are those who live for the things the world offers them. They love it; they crave its pleasures. Their love for it has expelled the love of the Father from their hearts. However, there are others who love the Father so much that all lesser affections have been expelled from their hearts by love for Him. These God-pleasers have a wonderful promise: "Anyone who does what pleases God will live forever."

"Do not love this world nor the things it offers you, for when you love the world, you do not have the love of the Father in you. For the world offers only a craving for physical pleasure, a craving for everything we see, and pride in our achievements and possessions. These are not from the Father, but are from this world. And this world is fading away, along with everything that people crave. But anyone who does what pleases God will live forever." 1 John 2:15-17 (NLT)

### 1-14
### Self-Denial And Fullness
I cannot empty myself of myself by self-denial without the fullness of Christ. With the fullness of Christ, my self comes to its proper place. He teaches me how to lose my self and find it in Him. We must learn that self-hatred is not the path forward. The goal is not the annihilation of the self into nirvana. The fullness of Christ can expel from us the parts of self that need to die and revive the essence of the true self to live like it has never lived.

"For of His fullness we have all received, and grace upon grace." John 1:16 (NASB)

### 1-15
### Practicing Restitution
Restitution is the act of restoring to another what has been lost or taken. It may involve making payment for stolen items. It takes responsibility for its trespasses; it does not justify them. It acknowledges the importance of relationships, and often restores them to be better than before. It offers heartfelt apologies, and does whatever it can to make things right or whole again. It is an expression of sincere repentance. Wise parents have used it to teach their own children when they have taken something that did not belong to them. It should be practiced under the guidance of the Spirit and under the umbrella of genuine repentance.

"Then Zacchaeus stood and said to the Lord, 'Look, Lord, I give half of my goods to the poor; and if I have taken anything from anyone by false accusation, I restore fourfold.' And Jesus said to him, 'Today salvation has come to this house, because he also is a son of Abraham'." Luke 19:8-9 (NKJV)

### 1-16
### Believe Into Me
John 3:16 is a believing that is more than a mental conviction. It is a belief (full trust) on which you stake your whole life. The NT word "believe in Christ" has been oversimplified. In the NT it carries the idea of "believe into." Try reading it that way for new insights. This is what Jesus is saying. "Believe into" means that we have come to the place that our life is in total solidarity with Christ. That is where our salvation is found. Paul came to that place when He said, "I am

crucified "with Christ" (Galatians 2:20). Those who are "in Christ" walk in the Spirit and not in the flesh (Romans 8:1-20). In Christ we are a new creation (2 Corinthians 5:17). In Christ is the blessing of Abraham (Galatians 3:14). Keep believing into Jesus and see how it will bring you to a deeper relationship with Him.

## 1-17
### Living Out Truth

We spend a lot of time being exact about theology and doctrine; this is important. However, we must remember that we can have our thought process off when our heart is right. I heard someone say years ago, "Some people's lives are better than their theology." The head and heart should go together, but none of us have perfect mental grasp of all truth. A teaching that makes the personal pursuit of holiness unnecessary falls short. Our theology should lead us to a life of holiness and Christlikeness, not away from it. Faithfulness to God (i.e. faith acting) is more revealing than our belief statements. Trusting trumps knowledge.

"This will continue until we all come to such unity in our faith and knowledge of God's Son that we will be mature in the Lord, measuring up to the full and complete standard of Christ." Ephesians 4:13 (NLT)

## 1-18
### Restlessness

Some of us have a built-in restlessness with which we have to deal. We are doers, always busy, goal driven; new ideas and tasks keep pulling us forward. We keep adding things to our to-do list, although it is still filled with unfinished tasks. We are driven. Our electronic devices tend to reinforce our restlessness. There is a spiritual fallout from this. It works against patience and silence; it is the enemy of waiting and meditation. Better and lasting things are done when we allow the Spirit to work with us and through us. This requires slowing down and pausing in His Presence.

Lord, help me to learn better how to wait, how to get out of my energy into Your energy. Teach me how to rest in You. Amen.

**1-19**
**Live The Cross Through Resurrection**
In the process of bearing your cross, always remember that the resurrection follows the cross. It was true for Him. It will be true for you. See your dark times through the lens of the resurrection. It is paradoxically possible to experience your cross and the power of the resurrection at the same time. I can testify that it is so. In our world death follows life. In God's world resurrection follows death. We should cling to resurrection hope in the midst of our crosses. Our present dying does not have the last word; resurrection does.

"Praise be to the God and Father of our Lord Jesus Christ! In his great mercy he has given us new birth into a living hope through the resurrection of Jesus Christ from the dead, and into an inheritance that can never perish, spoil or fade--kept in heaven for you, who through faith are shielded by God's power until the coming of the salvation that is ready to be revealed in the last time. In this you greatly rejoice, though now for a little while you may have had to suffer grief in all kinds of trials." 1 Peter 1:3-6 (NIV)

**1-20**
**Glory In The Cross**
It is easier to complain about our crosses than to glory in them. Paul gloried in the cross. "God forbid that I should glory, save in the cross of our Lord Jesus Christ, by whom the world is crucified unto me, and I unto the world" (Galatians 6:14 KJV). The cross is not simply shaping us into glory; the cross is glory. Praise God for your cross. Christ, the Glory of God, is to be found there. When we are crucified with Christ, God's glory rests upon us.

**1-21**
**The Church**
Some have concluded that the church does not matter anymore in the Christian's life. Let us pause and think about this. The church is the body of Christ of which we have become a baptized body member. It is the family of God into which we are adopted. It is the fellowship of saints that has made us partners in mission. It is the assembly of believers gathered to celebrate the Messiahship of Jesus to worship in word and sacrament. It is the bride of Christ being purified for the Groom. It is the remnant that God is saving from the earth. It is the new humanity demonstrating real human ways of being in the world. It is the New

Israel that is gathering Jew and Gentile into a new covenant people. Before you discard the church as unnecessary, think on these things

"The body is a unit, though it is made up of many parts; and though all its parts are many, they form one body. So it is with Christ. For we were all baptized by one Spirit into one body--whether Jews or Greeks, slave or free--and we were all given the one Spirit to drink." 1 Corinthians 12:12-13 (NIV)+

## 1-22
### As He Walked
We proclaim, "I am a Christian; I am not ashamed." It takes more than proclamation. "He who says he abides in Him ought himself also to walk just as He walked" (1 John 2:6 NKJV). To commit our lives to Christ is more than signing up for salvation. It is to study how He walked so that we can walk the same way. It is looking at how He coped with rejection, unfairness, abandonment, cursing, ridicule and crucifixion so we can handle it as He did. By His Spirit and in His strength it can be done.

## 1-23
### Self-Pity or Fruitful Ministry
We heal others out of our own brokenness. We comfort others with the comfort God has given us in our trials. We give grace out of our own wounds. Our weaknesses, failures, and handicaps do not excuse us from ministry, but make a way for it; this keeps us from ever being victims. Keep thinking and talking about all the bad things that have happened to you, and you will paralyze growth and dwell in the lowlands of sadness and self-pity. Minister out of those same hurts, without complaint, and you will come to live in a higher and happier dimension.

"Blessed be the God and Father of our Lord Jesus Christ, the Father of mercies and God of all comfort, who comforts us in all our affliction, so that we may be able to comfort those who are in any affliction, with the comfort with which we ourselves are comforted by God." 2 Corinthians 1:3-4 (ESV)

## 1-24
### Truth Pairs
These things are mutually exclusive: Worshiping God and worshiping idols, serving God and mammon, living in the flesh and living in the Spirit, loving the world and loving the Father. These things must go together: faith and works, trust and obedience, love and action, prayer and service, justification and sanctification, justice and righteousness, the cross and resurrection, the bread and the cup, patience and perseverance, truth and the Word, the written word and the Living Word, prayer and listening, heaven and earth. Think on these things.

## 1-25
### Yes, Lord!
Spiritual progress is a series of "Yeses" to the Lord. To say, "Yes" affirms His Lordship in our lives. To say, "No, Lord" is a contradiction. We are saved by confessing and living out "Jesus is Lord". There is an initial "Yes" that is reaffirmed by a lifetime of "Yeses". The first surrendering "Yes" nails it down and the rest of the "Yeses" entrench that surrender into character. Jesus says, "Follow me!", and our "Yes" is to follow. He says, "Deny yourself and take up your cross" and our "Yes" is to embrace the painful process. He says, "I will never leave you, nor forsake you," and our "Yes" is to trust the promise. Eve said, "No" to God. The virgin Mary said "Yes". That "Yes" made her fit to be the "God-bearer". Our "Yeses" take us into holiness as Christlikeness where we too become God-bearers.

"Then Mary said, 'Here am I, the servant of the Lord; let it be with me according to your word.' Then the angel departed from her." Luke 1:38 (NRSV)

## 1-26
### Live Life In This Moment
Life is empty without Christ filling this present moment. It is drudgery without the knowledge of Presence. It is sadness not yet walking with joy. It walks in grief as the two Emmaus' disciples did, not knowing that Resurrection was walking with them. The Jews looked back to salvation in the Exodus. Some only see salvation as future eschatology. The resurrection of Jesus has declared, "Now is the day of salvation!" Walking with Him saves the moments and makes each

moment saving. Walking with Resurrection changes the tense of hope from future to present as "living hope" (1 Peter 1:3).

For he says, "At an acceptable time I have listened to you, and on a day of salvation I have helped you." See, now is the acceptable time; see, now is the day of salvation! 2 Corinthians 6:2b (NRSV)

## 1-27
### Representing The Father
Father, may I never misrepresent You. May I show to others what You have shown me about Yourself. May I be as kind, loving and generous to others as You have been to me. May I be a mirror reflecting Who You really are to all of those who come into my life. May your Spirit in me reproduce Your life through me. May I rediscover that the way for this to occur in my life is to simply follow the Son. Amen!

"So Jesus said to them again, 'Peace be with you; as the Father has sent Me, I also send you.' And when He had said this, He breathed on them and said to them, 'Receive the Holy Spirit.'" John 20:21-22

## 1-28
### Choosing Our Attitude
We somehow think that our attitudes are mere spontaneous reactions to what is going on around us. We seldom think about choosing our attitude. We can meet harshness with harshness, hostility with hostility, but where does that get us? When we intentionally build into our personality humility, gentleness, kindness, love and caring, it will form a base for us to choose our attitudes aright. For the followers of Christ, these qualities are not optional, they are essential.

"You were taught, with regard to your former way of life, to put off your old self, which is being corrupted by its deceitful desires; to be made new in the attitude of your minds; and to put on the new self, created to be like God in true righteousness and holiness." Ephesians 4:22-24 (NIV)

## 1-29
### Prayer Beyond Feelings
Sometimes when we need to pray the most, we pray the least. Communication with God is the breath of the soul. It is availing ourselves of the very life of God. We may not always feel the difference, but the difference is there. We must get beyond praying only when we feel like it. Something is trained and changed in our inner being by prayer. It shifts our center of gravity. It orients temporal life to the Eternal God.

"Now He was telling them a parable to show that at all times they ought to pray and not to lose heart." Luke 18:1 (NASB)

## 1-30
### To Love Is To Overcome
"And because lawlessness will be increased, the love of many will grow cold. But the one who endures to the end will be saved" (Matthew 24:12-13 ESV). The crazier the world gets the harder it becomes to love one another. If we permit it, lawlessness, iniquity, and abounding sin have a way of putting the damper on love. This affects our endurance. The endurance expected here is the endurance of loving all people at all times and in all the ways we can. The saved are those who have endured to overcome the world by love.

## 1-31
### Greener Grass
We look for greener grass away from our present pasture. Looking somewhere else tends to destroy the present place. God has nourishment for us where we are. The Shepherd does lead us into green pastures and beside still waters, yet often we want Him to lead us "real soon" to a place that is better than where we are. Our Feeder (i.e. Shepherd) is with us in our life in this present moment and will lead us by His wisdom to the nourishment we need in His time.

"The LORD is my shepherd; I shall not want. He makes me lie down in green pastures. He leads me beside still waters. He restores my soul. He leads me in paths of righteousness for his name's sake. Even though I walk through the valley of the shadow of death, I will fear no evil, for you are with me; your rod and your staff, they comfort me. You prepare a table before me in the presence of my enemies; you anoint my head with oil; my cup overflows. Surely goodness and mercy shall follow me all the days of my life, and I shall dwell in the house of the LORD forever." Psalm 23:1-6 (ESV)

## 2-1
### Life's Problems
Life is full of difficult problems; we feel they are a curse. We believe that they should never be a part of life, however, we are here to deal with life with all of its problems, to deal with what we have been dealt. There are no solutions without problem solving. There is no overcoming without some obstacle to overcome. All of us do not have the same psychological tools to cope with our problems, but we all have grace available to help us if we will ask for it. The Spirit will help us through.

"Beloved, do not be surprised at the fiery trial when it comes upon you to test you, as though something strange were happening to you." 1 Peter 4:12 (ESV)

## 2-2
### The Pleasures of Sin
There are pleasures in sin for a season (Hebrews 11:25). The problem is that the pleasure becomes a part of the reward system of our psyche reaching literally into the very cells of our body. The pleasure that sin gives becomes intrenched in our cells in self-justifying ways that make it difficult for us to accept or want rescue or recovery. To be free means that we must hear the call of grace and start to want its energy. When we start to see sin's pleasures, not as treasures, but as chains, then we are on the way to rescue and recovery.

"Jesus replied, 'I tell you the truth, everyone who sins is a slave to sin...so if the Son sets you free, you will be free indeed.'" John 8:34, 36 (NIV)

## 2-3
### Pursued By Joy
Joy pursues us throughout our lives. Sometimes we will not allow it to catch us. We feel that our sorrows are too serous to experience joy; it would diminish or deny our pain, preventing us from feeling or working on the sad things. Not true! Life is not joy or sorrow; it is joy and sorrow. If you refuse the overtures of joy, waiting for no sorrow, you cheat yourself immeasurably. Joy is all around us. A

smile, a child, a game, a bird, a flower, a fragrance, a friend, a funny conversation, a sunset, a mountain, a stream, a meadow and much more. Then, there is the joy that comes from the Spirit. It is a special joy, for it has God's glory in it.

Oh, God of Abraham, Laughter* and Jacob, thank you for putting joy in our lives and on our trail. You have sent joy so we can "Go out with joy" (Isaiah 55:12) to meet life in the glad and sad ways it contains. Thank you, Father, for being at the very heart of our joy. Amen. *(Laughter is the meaning of Isaac's name.)

**2-4**
**Trust Is Central**
It is easier to make our belief systems about God more central in our life than God Himself. Mind you, beliefs are important; beliefs must go hand and hand with trust. Our lives are held steady by trusting God in all things. At the center of our lives there is to be a Person, full of kindness, gentleness and love in whom our trust can be unreservedly and unendingly placed. He is trustworthy, completely so. In trust there is relationship, fulfillment and the stability we need.

"How blessed is the man who has made the LORD his trust, And has not turned to the proud, nor to those who lapse into falsehood." Psalm 40:4 (NASB)

**2-5**
**Trust Is Deep**
Trusting God has surrender in it. It may be difficult for some to turn everything over to Him; trust is self-denying. Trust is a choice not for cowards; it takes courage to let go of my way of living and being in the world. There are always detours to trust that interpose themselves into our trying times; we are prone to fall back on all we know, our experiences and self-sufficiency. Trust Him fully; trust Him with everything. Trusting God is a part of loving Him. In love, hold on to Him with your whole being.

Father, forgive us of partial trust and may Your work deepen in us; we want to trust You wholeheartedly. Amen.

## 2-6
### Transforming Gratitude
Gratitude can be a huge turning point in our lives. God generously sends His unconditional love on all. He sends His rain on the just and on the unjust. Conversion is when the unjust get a vision of a God of unconditional love and fall before Him in gratitude and worship. Gratitude to our gracious Lord not only changes our circumstances, it transforms us.

"Therefore as you have received Christ Jesus the Lord, so walk in Him, having been firmly rooted and now being built up in Him and established in your faith, just as you were instructed, and overflowing with gratitude." Colossians 2:6-7 (NASB)

## 2-7
### Trust God
Trust Him when you do not understand, when you cannot figure it out, when you cannot figure Him out. Trust Him when you cannot see your way through, when it seems that He has abandoned you, when you want to give up. Trust Him when all the things you thought you knew about Him are being shaken. Trust Him when all your certainties have become less certain. Trusting God must be the central focal point to our lives and not merely our belief systems about Him.

"Trust in the LORD with all your heart; do not depend on your own understanding." Proverbs 3:5 (NLT)

## 2-8
### Practicing Truth
Probably one of the most challenging things we have to do is to practice what we preach and live the truth we endorse; it is a must. It requires connecting truth to life; it requires self-discipline. It prevents us from floating down stream. It sets us on a course to personally follow truth as opposed to merely espousing truth. The alternative to this is hypocrisy, and thus to sully the cause of truth by the lives we live. Living and practicing truth leads to real character development; it is to grow in holiness.

"The teachers of the law and the Pharisees sit in Moses' seat. So you must obey them and do everything they tell you. But do not do what they do, for they do not practice what they preach. They tie up heavy loads and put them on men's shoulders, but they themselves are not willing to lift a finger to move them." Matthew 23:2-4 (NIV)

## 2-9
### Playing The Devil
Some of us do not need the Accuser (Satan) since we can become our own accuser. Beating ourselves up over past decisions and actions only serves to abuse ourselves; it serves to destroy the present moment. The way out of this accusing cycle is to know that God loves us and has truly forgiven us. We cannot be taken in by accusing voices, be they Satan, other people, or even ourselves. We can say, "Get behind me Satan" by refusing to do his work for him.

Lord Jesus, thank You for the victory You won over the Accuser in the wilderness and finally on the cross. Teach us to resist the accusing voice by listening to the affirming voice of Your love, grace and mercy toward us. Amen!

## 2-10
### Sincerity And Authenticity
There is no growth in and toward holiness without being sincere. Authenticity is the outcome of sincerity. I can only press forward in the journey as I am honest with myself about myself. That is not easy. For me, it requires an ongoing confession and desire to turn from the things in myself that are unlike Him. I have found that, though I sincerely want to be like Him, I cannot arrive there without the grace and help of His Spirit. The Spirit is the Spirit of Christ, thus the Spirit alone can enable true Christlikeness.

Jesus, by Your Spirit, grant that I may pursue You in sincerity and truth. Expose any false way in me that I may worship You in truth. Amen!

## 2-11
### Faith As Faithfulness
"God's covenant justice comes into operation through the faithfulness of Jesus the Messiah, for the benefit of all who have faith" (Romans 3:22 KNT). In the NT the "faith of Jesus" is really better translated "the faithfulness of Jesus", as in this

translation. Notice it says, "for the benefit of all who have faith". Our faith joined to His faithfulness is saving faith. Living the New Covenant in faith means that we seek to be faithful to God in the same way Jesus has been faithful to us. Faithfulness is the proof of faith's presence.

2-12
### Christlike Settings
On our electronic devices we have default settings that cause the computer to behave in ways based on these settings. We also have default settings built into our personality by a lifetime of habits. Sometimes our settings can be anger, reactive, unkind, or even nasty and cruel, etc. The believer is in the process of changing the old default settings to Christlikeness. These settings are the fruit of the Spirit (Galatians 5:22-23a). The Spirit seeks our co-operation and we need to ask for His help.

"But the fruit of the Spirit is love, joy, peace, patience, kindness, goodness, faithfulness, gentleness, self-control" Galatians 5:22-23a (NASB).

2-13
### Worth And Value
The English word worthy has its roots in worth. We are prone to use the word worthy only in reference to the Lamb of God; certainly He alone was worthy to open the seven-sealed book. Yet Jesus said that the worthy are those who take up the cross and follow Him (Matthew 10:38). However, the fact is, God has declared our value in two ways by His own actions. He made us in His likeness, and He sent His Son to rescue us. Do not ever allow guilt and shame to turn off the overtures of love and grace. You have immeasurable value to Your Father.

2-14
### The Victory Of Light
"The light shines in the darkness, and the darkness can never extinguish it" (John 1:4-9 NLT). Jesus is the true Light. The darkness cannot put it out. The dark world cannot put it out; the dark heart cannot put it out. The Light has come to triumph over darkness. It has. It does. It will. Stop giving the darkness credit; cease letting it depress you. The One who said, "Let there be light" is Himself

the Light. The One who created suns, stars, moons and comets is the source of our illumination. In the culmination of all things, the Light wins.

"And there will be no more night; they need no light of lamp or sun, for the Lord God will be their light, and they will reign forever and ever" Revelation 22:5 (NRSV)

## 2-15
### For Your Good
Joseph said to his brothers, "You meant it to me for evil, but God meant it to me for good" (Genesis 50:20). What others design for your destruction, God can redesign for your salvation, and in the case of Joseph, salvation for the whole family. It is easy to become angry and frustrated when unfair things happen to us. Surrender it. Give it time. God will refine, mature and use you through your troubles.

Father, teach us how to surrender the actions of other people that have negatively impacted us. Help us to realize that You are working in all things to shape us like Your Son, reacting as He did when unfair things were poured upon Him. Amen!

## 2-16
### Collective Maturity
"Until all of us come to the unity of the faith and of the knowledge of the Son of God, to maturity, to the measure of the full stature of Christ" (Ephesians 4:13 NRSV). God designs that we come to maturity along with our brothers and sisters in the church. The gifts are for the growth of the body unit and for its unity. Christlikeness is to be the main outcome of body life. We come together to it and for it. Pure individualism will not get us there. We need each other to arrive at this maturity; we need the whole body to look like Jesus.

## 2-17
### Our Perfectionism
We want to be perceived as having it all together in some kind of perfect way. We can beat ourselves up when we don't. We can blame others for doing things that make us react in imperfect ways. Perfectionism can be frustrating,

debilitating, and depressing. No matter how good we did, it is never good enough. Cut yourself some slack! Remember, God loves us in spite of our shortcomings. Receiving grace should be a humble confession that we need something from God and others that we cannot supply with our own performance.

"And God is able to make all grace abound to you, so that always having all sufficiency in everything, you may have an abundance for every good deed." 2 Corinthians 9:8 (NASB)

## 2-18
### Time to Think

We live lives too busy for our own good health. Our culture and our devices keep us in their grip. We are driven from one thing to another. We don't lay one thing down until we have already picked up something else. Quietness and silence are hard to come by. We are too busy to listen and too busy speaking to hear. Both experience and research studies show that we all need quiet time and silence. These times of thinking and meditating give us perspective and get us back on the right track. Listen! He speaks!

"Finally, brothers, whatever is true, whatever is honorable, whatever is just, whatever is pure, whatever is lovely, whatever is commendable, if there is any excellence, if there is anything worthy of praise, think about these things. What you have learned and received and heard and seen in me—practice these things, and the God of peace will be with you." Philippians 4:8-9 (ESV)

## 2-19
### Love Transforms

Love transforms the receiver of love. We have been transformed by the love of God. We transform others by giving love. The truth is, people are made normal by love and become abnormal in the absence of it. This is certainly observable in the lives of healthy families and dysfunctional families. The crucifixion of Jesus was a rejection of His kingship by the world, yet it ironically was an act of redeeming love when He laid down His life for all. Since love has transformed us, we are commissioned to be change-agents, laying down our lives in love to transform others.

"For Christ's love compels us, because we are convinced that one died for all, and therefore all died. And he died for all, that those who live should no longer live for themselves but for him who died for them and was raised again."
2 Corinthians 5:14-15 (NIV)


## 2-20
### An Unlikely Trade`
Moses made a trade that most folks would not make. He traded pleasure for oppression and suffering. He rejected the pleasure benefits that could have been his; he moved from alignment with a world power to be identified with a band of slaves. In a pleasure-seeking culture such a choice seems crazy. Fleeting pleasures are often at the price of not being identified with the enslaved peoples of our world. Jesus came to suffer with the slaves and by suffering to free them.

"He (Moses) chose to share the oppression of God's people instead of enjoying the fleeting pleasures of sin. He thought it was better to suffer for the sake of Christ than to own the treasures of Egypt." Hebrews 11:25-26a (NLT)


## 2-21
### Human Need
Jesus would not allow religious traditions and rules about the Sabbath to get in the way of helping people (John 5:8-10). He repeatedly challenged these traditions. A priest and a Levite would not go out of their way to be contaminated by the blood of a robbery victim. It was a good Samaritan that came to the rescue. Our involvement in religious things must not get in the way of helping people. John Wesley said, "Acts of mercy take precedence over acts of piety." How can we really worship if we intentionally avoid human need and suffering?

"Jesus *said to him, 'Get up, pick up your pallet and walk.' Immediately the man became well, and picked up his pallet and began to walk. Now it was the Sabbath on that day. So the Jews were saying to the man who was cured, 'It is the Sabbath, and it is not permissible for you to carry your pallet.'" John 5:8-10 (NASB)

**2-22**
## Troubles And God's Will
The storm does not mean God did not send you, neither does rejection or even persecution. We think if we are in God's will there are never any downside consequences. Both OT and NT contradict that false notion. Think of Moses, David, Job, Jeremiah, Paul in prison or John on Patmos. Even Jesus, doing the will of God, was crucified. Difficulties do not suggest that we are out of God's will, but may confirm that we are in it. This world if full of suffering, and followers of Jesus are not immune from it.

"Immediately he made the disciples get into the boat and go before him to the other side, while he dismissed the crowds…but the boat by this time was a long way from the land, beaten by the waves, for the wind was against them." Matthew 14:22, 24 (ESV)

**2-23**
## Your Story Goes On
The end of your life is not the end of your story. Our story lives on in the lives of others long after we are gone. Our actions filter down through our descendants and through all of our human connections. All lives have immeasurable impact in either positive or negative ways. All persons change the world in more ways than we have acknowledged. Our lives produce fruit in those we have impacted. Our prayer is always that it will be good fruit. Our story is immortal when it finds itself in God's story. It is His story that gives meaning to our story.

Lord Jesus, Your story is the greatest story ever told. You reached down and lifted me up and forever changed my story. Thanks for including me in Your story. Help me to ever live Your story today and for generations not yet born. Amen!

**2-24**
## For the Sake of His Name
"He restores my soul: he leads me in the paths of righteousness for his name's sake" (Psalm 23:3). We ask Him to lead us and guide us (Psalm 31:3) and to forgive our sins (Psalm 79:9) for His name's sake. "Nevertheless he saved them for his name's sake, that he might make his mighty power to be known" (Psalm

106:8 KJV). "For the LORD will not cast away his people, for his great name's sake, because it has pleased the LORD to make you a people for himself" (1 Samuel 12:22 NRSV). "For the sake of His name", He does all of this and more. Why? He has taken upon Himself a vested interest in our redemption. He has put His name on the line. Grace without measure! Love unfathomable! Faithfulness beyond comprehension! Don't let His name down.

"Let everyone who names the name of Christ depart from iniquity." 2 Timothy 2:19b (NKJV)

## 2-25
### Self-Sufficiency
Self-sufficiency is something that is ingrained into our Western culture. It is a myth, quite demonstrably so. We cannot build a house, nor a life without the tools and experiences we have received from others. Self-sufficiency leads to self-dependance where we do not think that we need other people at all. We think we don't need God either, though we do. Stop and think about how other people have contributed to your life. Stop and think of how you need the sustaining grace of God every moment.

"Come now, you who say, 'Today or tomorrow we will go to such and such a city, and spend a year there and engage in business and make a profit.' Yet you do not know what your life will be like tomorrow. You are just a vapor that appears for a little while and then vanishes away. Instead, you ought to say, 'If the Lord wills, we will live and also do this or that.' But as it is, you boast in your arrogance; all such boasting is evil." James 4:13-16 (NASB)

## 2-26
### Sackcloth And Ashes (Ash Wednesday)
"Then I turned to the Lord God, to seek an answer by prayer and supplication with fasting and sackcloth and ashes" (Daniel 9:3 NRSV). Coarse sackcloth does not make for a comfortable suit. We don't wear burlap cloth to go about our day. We dress in more comfortable attire. However, Daniel laid aside his nice clothes for some serious prayer, covering himself with ashes. He was seeking an answer. It was real "prayer and supplication", down-to-business praying! There are times of urgency in our lives when conversational prayer gives way to intense prayer sessions.

## 2-27
### Close The Door
"When you pray, go away by yourself, shut the door behind you, and pray to your Father in private. Then your Father, who sees everything, will reward you" (Matthew 6:6 NLT). Shutting the door is about shutting distracting things out as preparation for talking to our Father. We have all tried leaving the door open and things come in. It takes discipline and focus to close the door. But when we realize that the whole point of closing the door is to be with our beloved Father, then it becomes a necessity.

## 2-28
### The Sadness Room
You may live with a room in your heart called sadness. There are no walls around this room, only a vapor barrier that does not always hold. You learn to know that it is there; you respect its presence, never denying it. But you also learn that it is not always safe to go there; it can be debilitating. You live knowing that a changing breeze in the house can push it stiflingly close. There is a cross hanging in the main room, and as you pray and surrender, sadness drifts toward the cross to the point they are nearly indistinguishable. In that moment you have given it one more time to Jesus; you open a window and a settled serenity comes in and you see rays of joy coming from the Risen Son.

"Cast your burden on the LORD, and he will sustain you" Psalm 55:22a

## 2-29
### Rely on God
It is so easy for us to rely on lots of things besides God. We have a desire for self-sufficiency and independence. We want to be on our own. "Therefore let him who thinks he stands take heed that he does not fall" (1 Corinthians 10:12, NASB). We must rely fully on God and not our own wisdom, our training, our life experiences, our positive attitude, our resources, our stoicism, nor our strong will. Unless the Lord builds our spiritual house, we labor in vain (Ps 127:1).

## 3-1
### Fixing Folks
We cannot fix other people. We can love them. Love, when received, has a way of doing the fixing. What makes us want to fix the flaws in other people when we have a basket full of our own? What makes us want to control a person with free will, when God does not even do that? Control carries with it bondage. Love invites us to freedom.

Lord Jesus, thank You for Your love that frees us to be what we were intended to be. Thank You for the freedom Your Love has birthed in us. Amen.

## 3-2
### Timing and Hearing
Jesus said, "I have many things to say to you but you cannot bear it now" (John 16:12). There are times and places in our lives that we can't hear what we may need to hear. Sometimes we look back on our lives and wish we could have heard something that we came to understand later; the reality is, we were not necessarily ready at that point in our journey to know. We needed a few more life experiences, a little more maturity, to get there. Now that the Spirit has come, He can keep us up to date in what we need to receive now.

"But when he, the Spirit of truth, comes, he will guide you into all truth. He will not speak on his own; he will speak only what he hears, and he will tell you what is yet to come." John 16:13 (NIV)

## 3-3
### Know God Better
If you want to know God better, walk in obedience to Him. If you want to know the will of God for your life, then live your life according to His will revealed in the teachings of Jesus. Stop trying to use God for the things that you want to receive. Learn to be with Him without asking. Make your times with Him more about worship, thanking and praising than anything else. It will surprise you what you will learn about your Father.

"Your Father knows what you need before you ask him." Matthew 6:8

## 3-4
### Purpose and Meaning
Do you want to find purpose and meaning? Serve those whom God has placed in your life. Do you want to find yourself? Then lose yourself. Do you want to get to the top? Go to the bottom and serve. Stop living to receive and live to give. Start celebrating the good things in the lives of others. We seldom find the meaning of life in isolation from people around us. We do not even acquire an identity for ourselves apart from the people with whom we have associated. Purpose is found in mission and serving.

"Whoever wishes to save his life will lose it, but whoever loses his life for My sake, he is the one who will save it." Luke 9:24 (NASB)

## 3-5
### Cruciform Living
Looking at the cross as a place where Jesus died for me is foundational, but it is not the whole house. Growth in grace requires that we move beyond seeing the cross as the place Jesus died for us and begin to see it as the place we die with Him. Thanking God for the cross is one thing, but getting on it with our Lord is to take gratitude to a new level. Cruciform living is the life to which we have been called.

"Do you not know that all of us who have been baptized into Christ Jesus were baptized into his death? We were buried therefore with him by baptism into death, in order that, just as Christ was raised from the dead by the glory of the Father, we too might walk in newness of life." Romans 6:3-4 (ESV)

## 3-6
### Second Chance
Father, thank you for a new day. Amen! Every day is a second chance to redeem time. It is an opportunity to express the love of Christ to another; it is an opportunity to give grace to a stranger. It is a new day to show patience and kindness; it is a second chance to show grace. We must not allow the sins of our past to define us; we are to declare every day as a new day to follow our Lord and walk the way His example shows us.

"Be careful then how you live, not as unwise people but as wise, making the most of the time, because the days are evil." Ephesians 5:15-16 (NRSV)

## 3-7
### Man Of Clay
"Then the LORD God formed man of dust from the ground" (Genesis 2:7). God takes a little dust, makes clay and makes a man. This God gets His hands dirty with humankind, again and again, but is still committed to the whole human race. Look at this commitment in Jesus. "All things were made through him, and without him was not any thing made that was made...the Word was made flesh" (John 1:3, 14). Jesus, who made a man of clay, became a man of clay. The heavenly became earthly that we could become heavenly (1 Corinthians 15:42-49). New creation! On the great resurrection morning, our new creation body will be just like Jesus' resurrected body. Stick to the Man of Clay; we are going somewhere. In Him we have a future and a hope. Hallelujah!

## 3-8
### The Marriage of Peace and Gratitude
"Let the peace of Christ rule in your hearts, to which indeed you were called in one body; and be thankful" (Colossians 3:15 NASB). We have been invited to the peace that belongs to the body of Christ. The Greek word for peace here is the word from which we get undisturbed (irenic). Having been incorporated into His body we are to let the peace of Messiah rule our hearts, sit on the throne of our lives. Know that this peace, this undisturbed center, has been married to gratitude. There is no peace without being thankful. Thankfulness keeps Christ as our calm center.

## 3-9
### Loving The Flawed
You do not have to be flawless to walk with Jesus nor work for Him. His love is not conditioned on us being flawless. He does not pretend you are perfect by looking at you through His Son. He is not self-deceived. This theory is based on the premise that a perfect God can only love the perfect/holy. No! A thousand times, No! He received sinners. He ate with them. He went to parties with them. He loves us in spite of our imperfections. He who commands us to love

the flawed, even our enemies, has already practiced what He is asking us to do. He loves flawed me; He loves flawed thee.

"For while we were still helpless, at the right time Christ died for the ungodly. For one will hardly die for a righteous man; though perhaps for the good man someone would dare even to die. But God demonstrates His own love toward us, in that while we were yet sinners, Christ died for us." Romans 5:6-8 (NASB)

## 3-10
### Chosen
I did not choose my DNA, my skin color, my birth family, my tribe, my hometown, my first school, my first church, my country, and much more. This was what life dealt me. There was something I was given: I was made in the divine likeness; I was created as an object of God's love. So many things I did not and could not choose, yet I know in my heart of hearts that I am chosen. I am chosen by my Father, beloved by Him as His own child. I am an heir of His, made possible by my Elder Brother, Christ Himself.

"For you did not receive a spirit of slavery to fall back into fear, but you have received a spirit of adoption. When we cry, "Abba! Father!" it is that very Spirit bearing witness with our spirit that we are children of God, and if children, then heirs, heirs of God and joint heirs with Christ." Romans 8:15-17a (NRSV)

## 3-11
### Proclaim The Kingdom
The Kingdom of God has come. Jesus is its King. We are in it. We are sent from it. We are invited to it. We are citizens of it. We are ambassadors for it. The actions of the Kingdom are as imperceptible as yeast in dough. It may appear as insignificant as a tiny mustard seed. It is a sower going out to sow. It is a wide net pulling in fish. It is a vineyard with a master vine dresser. It is a treasure in a field; it is a pearl that you would give all to obtain. The world desperately needs this upside-down, peaceable kingdom. Go announce the good news of the kingdom.

"This gospel of the kingdom shall be preached in the whole world as a testimony to all the nations, and then the end will come." Matthew 24:14

## 3-12
### "If Only..."
We sort out the past in some very unhealthy ways. We say, "If I only I had..." "If only I had not..." We feel bad about how a choice of ours influenced someone else. It is true that our actions intermingle with other people's choices. We all make mistakes and misspeak in all the relationships of life. When it happens to us we should give grace. Also we should extend/receive grace for ourselves in these things. In the end we are not responsible for other people's choices, though we may feel guilt for any part we might have played. Our Father is full of abounding grace and tender compassion for us. To be enfolded in that is hopeful and healing.

"The LORD is like a father to his children, tender and compassionate to those who fear him. For he knows how weak we are; he remembers we are only dust." Psalm 103:13-14 (NLT)

## 3-13
### Touching Sinners
The pharisees feared that their "holiness" would be contaminated by involvement with sinners-the unclean. The holiness of Jesus sought to be involved with sinners=the unclean, so that a loving/holy touch might be make them clean. He touched the leper (Matthew 8:2) and went to the home of a leper (Matthew 26:6); no pharisee would ever have done that. This is why Jesus said that He did not come to condemn but to rescue. Condemning others does not establish our righteousness nor holiness. Besides, condescending-condemning speeches push them away. We need to get over our pharisaical holiness and embrace the holiness of Jesus and start touching and healing the broken. Our broken world desperately needs that. Politics can never fix it. Seminars cannot. Holiness, with a tender touch, full embrace and unconditional love can.

## 3-14
### Light For Everyone
"The Word gave life to everything that was created, and his life brought light to everyone...The one who is the true light, who gives light to everyone, was coming into the world (John 1:4, 9 NLT)." The Word is the universal Light for everyone everywhere. Some have seen it and do not know its Name. Some have not seen it but can if they are shown. The Jesus who said, "I am the Light of

the world" also said "You are the light of the world." He taught that our light is good deeds done only to glorify our Father. Christians are the city on the hill whenever they can keep their self-centered baskets from hiding the light.

"You are the light of the world—like a city on a hilltop that cannot be hidden. No one lights a lamp and then puts it under a basket. Instead, a lamp is placed on a stand, where it gives light to everyone in the house. In the same way, let your good deeds shine out for all to see, so that everyone will praise your heavenly Father." Matthew 5:14-16 (NLT)

### 3-15
### Getting Close To God
"Come close to God, and God will come close to you. Wash your hands, you sinners; purify your hearts, for your loyalty is divided between God and the world" (James 4:8 NLT). God wants to be close to us. He has demonstrated it in the gift of His Son and His Spirit. His disposition toward us is not in question, therefore, we are invited to "Come close to Him". When coming near we must look at our hands and our heart. Hands contaminated by sinful actions must be cleansed; a divided heart must be purified. We cannot draw near when there is disobedience and divided loyalty. Deal with everything that keeps you from drawing close and then draw near.

### 3-16
### Sheep and Goats
In the final division between the sheep and goats, we want to be among the sheep (Matthew 25). If we do, then start by following the Lamb. The Lamb taught us to love our enemies, to forgive those who sin against us, to go the second mile, to give away our coat, to treat others like we would like to be treated, to feed the hungry, give water to the thirsty, clothe the naked, visit the sick and imprisoned, bless the one who curses us, pray for the spiteful, be a peace maker, etc. Follow the Lamb and we will finish the race well.

### 3-17
### The Ebenezer Stone
Setting up the Ebenezer stone marked a milestone in God's help. "Then Samuel took a stone and set it up between Mizpah and Jeshanah, and named it

Ebenezer; for he said, 'Thus far the LORD has helped us'" (1 Samuel 7:12 NRSV). The Lord Who has helped His people thus far is not about to abandon them now. He who started a good work in us wants to see it finished. He is faithful. He has been faithful. He will be faithful. You can bank on it. So set up your Ebenezer Stone.

"Here I raise my Ebenezer; Hither by Thy help I've come; And I hope, by Thy good pleasure, Safely to arrive at home." Robert Robinson

## 3-18
### Inclusion And Exclusion
"You have heard that it was said, 'Love your neighbor and hate your enemy.' But I tell you: Love your enemies…" (Matthew 5:43-44a). "Love your neighbor" was in the OT but "hate your enemy" was not; the saying was assumed to be true. If neighbors were included then enemies must be excluded. To get around "Love your neighbor" created an interpretation debate of, "Who is my neighbor?" (Luke 10:29). Jesus taught that your neighbor is anyone in need (Luke 10:29-37), but it did not stop there, it extended to "your enemies". Our Lord is not into excluding anyone from love, but including all as objects of love. That's what our Father does and that is what we are to do (Matthew 5:43-48). He who included us does not want us to exclude anyone that He loves, and that is everybody.

## 3-19
### Left Out
It is easy to look at others and rule them out of our favor because of a flaw, foible or failure. We are sometimes guilty of telling our "ain't-it-awful" stories about them. Whenever we rule others as unacceptable or unworthy we have set ourselves up as a false god, ruling on who is in and who is out. When we do, we become very much unlike the God who is. The true God loves us unconditionally in spite of our warts, failures and sins. We are forever drawing circles to keep away certain categories of people. Jesus drew a love circle around the whole globe. If He had not, you and I would have been left out.

"The Lord is not slow in keeping his promise, as some understand slowness. He is patient with you, not wanting anyone to perish, but everyone to come to repentance." 2 Peter 3:9 (NIV)

**3-20**
## Hidden With Christ In God
"You have died, and your life is hidden with Christ in God" (Colossians 3:3). Our union with Christ is more than walking the path with Him. When He died we died with Him. When He rose we rose with Him. God is in Christ, Christ is in God, and we are concealed with Christ in God. We now live the hidden-with-Christ-in-God life, mystical but real. This is a transforming union that is not escapism; it teaches us how to live right in this present world.

"If then you have been raised with Christ, seek the things that are above, where Christ is, seated at the right hand of God. Set your minds on things that are above, not on things that are on earth. For you have died, and your life is hidden with Christ in God. When Christ who is your life appears, then you also will appear with him in glory." Colossians 3:1-4 (ESV)

**3-21**
## Revealing The Concealed
At the great appearing of Jesus Christ, those whose lives have been hidden with Christ in God will appear with Him. Those who died with Him and rose with Him will come back with Him. The hidden-with-Christ-in-God people anticipate an awesome future. Those whose lives have been concealed with Him will be revealed with Him. The coming of our Lord Jesus will be with all His saints (I Thessalonians 3:13). Since we are coming back with Him, keep nurturing your hidden life with Him. "For the creation waits with eager longing for the revealing of the children of God" (Romans 8:19).

"If then you have been raised with Christ, seek the things that are above, where Christ is seated at the right hand of God. Set your minds on things that are above, not on things that are on earth. For you have died, and your life is hidden with Christ in God. When Christ who is your life appears, then you also will appear with him in glory." Colossians 3:1-4 (ESV)

**3-22**
## Watch Your Focus
"Set your minds on things that are above, not on things that are on earth" (Colossians 3:2). What you focus on will break you or shape you. It can make you whole or make you unhealthy. It can make you sane or crazy. It can

bring you to a new and better place or it can leave you in despair. We can focus on our decaying body or we can focus on inner renewal. We can be dragged around by the temporal or we can hook our wagon to the eternal. Turn your eyes upon Jesus!

"Therefore we do not lose heart, but though our outer *person* is decaying, yet our inner *person* is being renewed day by day. For momentary, light affliction is producing for us an eternal weight of glory far beyond all comparison, while we look not at the things which are seen, but at the things which are not seen; for the things which are seen are temporal, but the things which are not seen are eternal." 2 Corinthians 4:16-18

**3-23**
**We Must Continue**
We were alienated from God, even hostile in mind, loving the world and its evil deeds, when we were reconciled by Jesus. The reconciled are called to make their lives an offering that is holy, blameless and above reproach to their Lord. How can those who were such sinners be made holy? Paul said that it is by continuing in the faith. Demas, a coworker was with Paul at the time of this letter (Colossians 4:14). Later Paul would write, "Demas has forsaken us, having loved this present world" (2 Timothy 4:10). What a sad legacy, shifting from "the hope of the gospel" to the love of the world. Oh my brothers and sisters, hear the words, "if indeed you continue in the faith" (v. 23). We must continue in faith, stable faith, steadfast faith, non-shifting faith, hope-of-the-gospel faith (v. 23). We must! By grace, we can!

"And you, who once were alienated and hostile in mind, doing evil deeds, he has now reconciled in his body of flesh by his death, in order to present you holy and blameless and above reproach before him, if indeed you continue in the faith, stable and steadfast, not shifting from the hope of the gospel that you heard, which has been proclaimed in all creation under heaven, and of which I, Paul, became a minister." Colossians 1:21-23 (ESV)

**3-24**
**Tasting Fragrance**
If you could capture the fragrance of a flower and put it in a jar, it would be called honey. We are not able to do that, but the Creator is. He uses His servants the

bees to accomplish this amazing feat. The promised land was a land "flowing with milk and honey". If honey flows in abundance, then flowers must bloom in abundance. Liquid fragrance you can taste is why we like honey. "O taste and see that the LORD is good; How blessed is the man who takes refuge in Him!" (Psalm 34:10 NASB). Jesus is our Honey in the Rock. His aroma is pleasing and His fragrance is taste-able. He satisfies the soul.

"But I would feed you with the finest of the wheat, And with honey from the rock I would satisfy you." Psalm 81:16 (NASB)

## 3-25
### Unique Praise
Because we are made like no one else, we can bring glory and honor to God like no one else. We do, and should learn from each other, but we are not to be a copy of anyone else. We sometimes struggle when we are trying to get answers to our personal problems. The praying and grappling to apply the Word to our problems builds character and develops us in unique ways. This creates our unique story with a unique praise to our Lord.

Father, forgive us for sometimes disliking the fact that we are different. Teach us how to use our "different" to serve You and thus bring honor to You. Amen!

## 3-26
### Jonah Couldn't Swallow It
National and civil religion always tends to shut out those who do not fall in the boundaries of our particular nation. The ancient lands had their own national gods. Some in Israel thought of their God that way. God would have none of it. At a point in history the Assyrians had been cruel terrorist to the people of God; Israel hated them with an intense personal hatred. So God sent Jonah to preach to them. It horrified Jonah who went in the opposite direction. We have missed the story of Jonah over the debate of "can a man be swallowed by a fish and live?" That is not the point. It was not what swallowed Jonah, but what Jonah would not swallow. It was hard for Jonah to share a message of repentance from His compassionate God with enemies and aliens. God is still wanting to teach us to be as compassionate as our God is.

"Then the LORD said, 'You had compassion on the plant for which you did not work and which you did not cause to grow, which came up overnight and perished overnight. Should I not have compassion on Nineveh, the great city in which there are more than 120,000 persons who do not know the difference between their right and left hand, as well as many animals?'"   Jonah 4:10-11 (NASB)


## 3-27
### Like Abba
Many of my relatives and friends remind me of how much I look like my Dad. I bear his facial features, his mannerisms, and his physical infirmities in ways I keep discovering. I am thankful for the earthly father I had. I pray that I will also develop the beautiful characteristics of my Heavenly Abba. May His love find a path without resistance through my life. May He count on me to show His kind of grace and His kind of mercy to those whose lives intersect mine. May my earthly DNA be reshaped by the DNA of my Heavenly Father. I know what that looks like because I have seen it in my Elder Brother, Jesus.


## 3-28
### Children Of Abraham
In the NT age the Jewish people wanted to boast that they were descendants of Abraham. They debated who was and who was not. Paul saw the faith of Abraham was the mark of the sons of Abraham. James saw that the works of Abraham were a key to being of Abrahamic stock. It seemed that father Abraham had a rugged obedience to believe that God could raise Isaac from the dead. He could look at the uncountable stars to be like his descendants, even before he had a child. He could see the hills and valleys eventually being filled with them. He also messed up from time to time in getting ahead of God and lying to protect himself. This says, God can make imperfect folks children of Abraham too.


## 3-29
### You Belong Here
If God had weighed my flaws, numbered my sins, counted my selfish ways, and reckoned my deceit then I would be "without hope and without God" now and forever. I was far from Him because of my sin. I was far from being a

descendent of Israel. I was on the outside looking in, wondering what would happen to me, when He opened a door called mercy, hinged on grace. It swung wide open and I found myself enveloped by love that said, "You too belong here."

"Remember that you were at that time separate from Christ, excluded from the commonwealth of Israel, and strangers to the covenants of promise, having no hope and without God in the world. But now in Christ Jesus you who formerly were far off have been brought near by the blood of Christ." Ephesians 2:12-13 (NASB)

## 3-30
### Loss of Soul
A secular society cannot silence the spiritual essence of our being. A self-originating universe leaves us empty. We only push God out to our ultimate depravation. We do not do well when we forget God. We lose the ability to thrive. God is the great "I am". His handiwork is everywhere from the farthest galaxy to the nearest microbe. His mark is on our being. Discover Him and you will find your own soul; in that discovery you will find real life.

"You have made us for yourself Oh God, and our hearts are restless until they rest in Thee." St. Augustine

## 3-31
### The Destination Is Jesus
"If I go and prepare a place for you, I will come again and receive you to Myself, that where I am, there you may be also" (John 14:3). Hear it, "Where I am, there you may be also." Jesus is the reward; it is not heaven, a crown, nor a city with gold streets. Jesus is the heavenly place. He is our home. He is the desired destination. Every other desire is some form of idolatry. Oh, there will be a "place", but He is what makes "home" home. Without Him it is an empty house. When we are with Him it creates the place; our eyes are not on the place but on His face.

## 4-1
### Learning Humility Late
I wish I had learned more humility earlier. I am still learning. I did not know as much as I thought I knew. I thought myself right, when I later discovered my

attitude was wrong. The most difficult thing that I have had to learn is to face my true self. Sometimes when I see me in the Spirit's mirror it breaks my heart, it humbles me, it calls me to a new and deeper repentance. Oh Lord, I bow before You asking You to rescue me in new, deeper and saving ways. Amen!

"The humble He guides in justice, And the humble He teaches His way." Psalm 25:9 (NKJV)

## 4-2
### Loveless Imitations

We have grown up around spiritual people. We have heard their testimonies. We can observe their lives. We can deeply admire them. We can adopt their words and jargon, thinking that somehow it has become our own. We may go through certain steps that they said they went through. We may even think that we have arrived where they were because we are saying all the right things. But in the end we may become loveless imitations of the genuine. Without the love that fulfills true spirituality we end up in a kind of spiritual delusion. It will take much repentance to bring us out of such a place. Brokenness, humility, rejection of pride and deep cries for mercy can bring us to a place of genuineness and authentic love.

"Beloved, let us love one another, for love is from God; and everyone who loves is born of God and knows God. The one who does not love does not know God, for God is love." 1 John 4:7-8 (NASB)

## 4-3
### Silent Offerings

There are unnoticed silent offerings to God. Secret giving to others is rewarded openly (Matthew 6:2-4). Why does God bless us for what we do for others? What we do for the Father's children is deemed done to the Father. These silent offerings are unnoticed by others, yet the Father takes note of it and gives a blessing. Charity for the Christian is not about altruism, nor the feeling you might receive from that, but it is about giving offerings to the Father.

"God is not unjust; he will not forget your work and the love you have shown him as you have helped his people and continue to help them" (Hebrews 6:10 NIV).

## 4-4
### Compassion And Healing
Jesus had a very wide healing ministry (Matthew 4:24, 9:35). It was driven by the compassion He had for people. Jesus engaged the broken as a means of bringing wholeness. Jesus was not isolated from the world with its sin and sinners. He sat with them. He ate with them. He listened to them. He did not condemn them. His love for them drew them to the redemption that they so desperately needed. We have sold our souls for the scientific methodology of "church growth". The "methods" of Jesus defy methodology and are not methods at all. They are a way of being with fellow humans for their healing. It will be the salvation of them and the church if we will but return to it.

## 4-5
### The Stones Know Jesus
The disciples shouted out their loud praise to Jesus on Palm Sunday. The Pharisees protested this messianic proclamation. Jesus responded, "If they keep quiet, the stones will cry out." Figurative? I don't think so. In the OT stone monuments were erected as a testimony. No, more than that. Even stones are made of moving particles, sustained by their Creator Jesus. All the rays and particles of the universe know Jesus, because everything is generated and sustained by Him. Isn't it time to start lifting your praise to God's promised Messiah?

"Blessed is the king who comes in the name of the Lord!" "Peace in heaven and glory in the highest!" Some of the Pharisees in the crowd said to Jesus, "Teacher, rebuke your disciples!" "I tell you," he replied, "if they keep quiet, the stones will cry out." Luke 19:38-40 (NIV)

## 4-6
### Incarnation's Promise
When God became man, it was more than a historical event; it was a hint of a new future for mankind. When Heaven came down in Jesus, He immersed Himself in the life of earth; it was the anticipation of the final renewal of all things. Even His healing ministry anticipated a future where there is no disease. Incarnation was a piece of our future made present, heaven and earth becoming one. Incarnation promises that something has happened that will give rise to New Creation. We see it in His resurrected body, when an earthly body takes on

heavenly features. All things will change, according to the promise of incarnation and resurrection. There is now a solid reason that the future has hope.

## 4-7
### Injustice That Saved
Jesus was crucified unjustly by His religious and political persecutors, yet He used that injustice to justify sinners. He was thrown away as a worthless thing, but through the cross He goes looking for all the lost and abandoned. He was witnessed against by those who bore false witness, yet that falseness revealed Him to be truth. They showed Him no mercy, but His cross is the greatest act of mercy and grace the world has ever seen. They all meant it for evil, but God who works good out of all things, declared it a sin offering by which evil persons could be made good. They thought it was their power that took His life, but He had the real power to lay it down.

## 4-8
### Counted As A Transgressor
"He was numbered with the transgressors. For he bore the sin of many, and made intercession for the transgressors" (Isaiah 53:12). He was seen as just one more evil man and was "numbered with the transgressors", merely another executed criminal! The crucifiers very intentionally stuck Him between two thieves; from that center cross He did not retaliate against anyone, but bore the sins of humanity. It did not stop there; He makes intercession for transgressors even now. He became one with sinners in order to make us one with Him. Hallelujah, what A Savior!

## 4-9
### It Was Our Sins
The suffering of Christ was so great on the cross, that when we looked at it we thought it had to be God who did it; "We thought his troubles were a punishment from God, a punishment for his own sins!" But this is our denial, our failure to take responsibility for our own sinful actions. "But he was pierced for our rebellion, crushed for our sins." Our sins crucified Him, and still do. Our sins killed Him and in His great mercy He bore them far away. The cross expresses the pure love of God (Father, Son and Spirit) (John 3:16). It is love so great that it saves the crucifiers.

"He was despised and rejected— a man of sorrows, acquainted with deepest grief. We turned our backs on him and looked the other way. He was despised, and we did not care. Yet it was our weaknesses he carried; it was our sorrows that weighed him down. And we thought his troubles were a punishment from God, a punishment for his own sins! But he was pierced for our rebellion, crushed for our sins. He was beaten so we could be whole. He was whipped so we could be healed. All of us, like sheep, have strayed away. We have left God's paths to follow our own. Yet the LORD laid on him the sins of us all." Isaiah 53:3-6 (NLT)

## 4-10
### Beautiful Mystery
How could Jesus be David's son and yet David's Lord? He was! How could the Creator join the dust of the created? He did! How could He who was a descendent of Abraham be the "I Am" before Abraham? He is! How could the son of Mary be before Mary? He was! How could the One who died be the Resurrection and the Life? He is! How did the Creator of oceans, rivers and springs say, "I Thirst"? He did! How could the benevolent Lord of all submit Himself to corrupt leaders to be mocked, tried and executed? He did! How could the One from all eternity enter human pain, suffering and death? He did! How could He turn a Roman cross into an altar of sacrifice and redeem all creation with it? He did! How can blood shed over 2,000 years ago release us from our sins? It does! How could a thing as ugly as a cross become a thing of beauty? Oh, but it is!

Oh Christ, Mystery of God, Beautiful Savior, Lord of All, Shepherd of Israel, God with Us, Love from eternity, we love You; we adore You. We worship You, Oh, Holy One! Amen and Amen!

## 4-11
### Not A Ray Of Light
"If you are walking in darkness, without a ray of light, trust in the LORD and rely on your God" (Isaiah 50:10b NLT). Have you ever been there? It is not fun. It can be unnerving and downright frightening. Is there hope? How will I get out? Dark night of the soul! Give up? Never! Hold on? Yes! These are times we rely on the Lord with naked faith; they are times that we hold on to a hand that we

cannot see and believe in One whom we may not feel at the moment. We endure tomb-wait-time because we believe our Lord's name is Resurrection.

## 4-12
### Death Is Defeated
The women went looking for the dead crucified Jesus and found the tomb empty. They learned that He was alive. Death did not have the final word on Jesus and it does not have the final word on those who believe in Him. By His death He trampled down death; by His death the old enemy death lost its sting. This Resurrection Day declares that all tombs of the saints will one day open. Tomb time will give way to the bliss and glory of God's great tomorrow; it will be glorious beyond our most vivid imagination.

Jesus said to her, "I am the resurrection and the life. Whoever believes in me, though he die, yet shall he live, and everyone who lives and believes in me shall never die. Do you believe this?" John 11:25-26 (ESV)

## 4-13
### Women And Resurrection
Never forget that the first ones to announce the resurrection were women. This was in a time when women were not considered reliable witnesses in court. Yet Jesus flips human culture on its head and reveals Himself first to women. They go out as the first evangels to proclaim the resurrection of the Son of God. The men finally had to acknowledge that these God appointed women were declaring the truth and had been given the right to do so.

"Moreover, some women of our company amazed us. They were at the tomb early in the morning, and when they did not find his body, they came back saying that they had even seen a vision of angels, who said that he was alive. Some of those who were with us went to the tomb and found it just as the women had said, but him they did not see." Luke 24:22-24 (ESV)

## 4-14
### All Things Changed
The resurrection of Jesus changes everything. It changed history. The sting of death is replaced by the infusion of Life. It charged believers with hope. The

resurrection is the promise of new creation through Him who was the firstborn from the dead. The resurrection affirms atonement for sin is completed. We are forgiven. We are redeemed. We are born from above. We are citizens of the Kingdom. Our future is as bright as the resurrection of Jesus declares it to be.

"And from Jesus Christ, the faithful witness, the firstborn of the dead, and the ruler of the kings of the earth. To Him who loves us and released us from our sins by His blood." Revelation 1:5 (NASB)

## 4-15
### The Ultimate Ruler And Government
"On his robe and on his thigh he has a name written, King of kings and Lord of lords" (Revelation 19:16 ESV). We have not yet grasped the huge political implications of Jesus being King and of His government (i.e. Kingdom). The Romans saw their Caesars as immortal sons of God. Jesus demonstrated by His own resurrection that He alone was Lord. The lords and kings have a Lord and King; He is Jesus. The other governments of earth will become like the dust of the summer threshing floor (Daniel 2:35). Our focus on the governments of men can eclipse our vision of the Kingdom of God. Our focus on the Kingdom of God will put the passing politics and government of men in their rightful place. He alone is "the ruler of the kings of the earth" (Revelation 1:5).

"He who is the blessed and only Sovereign, the King of kings and Lord of lords, who alone possesses immortality and dwells in unapproachable light, whom no man has seen or can see. To Him be honor and eternal dominion! Amen."
1 Timothy 6:15b-16 (NASB)

## 4-16
### Walking With Resurrection
The two sad and brokenhearted disciples of Emmaus were walking the road of despair. The resurrected One joined them on this walk. How many times do we walk in sadness forgetting that we are walking with Resurrection? To remember that He is with us is to have the perspective of our saddest day changed. Remind yourself today that He is with you on your sad roads, your lonely roads, and your painful roads. You walk no road by yourself anymore.

"But they urged Him, saying, "Stay with us, for it is getting toward evening, and the day is now nearly over." So He went in to stay with them. When He had reclined at the table with them, He took the bread and blessed it, and breaking it, He began giving it to them. Then their eyes were opened and they recognized Him; and He vanished from their sight." Luke 24:29-31 (NASB)

## 4-17
### Joy And Unconditional Love

When we hold persons as unworthy of our love it impinges on our own happiness and joy. Listing other's flaws and foibles is seen as justification to not love. A measuring stick for other folks to get "our love" marks us as people who do not understand the great love God has for us. Anyway, it is not "our love" that we are to give away, it is the same kind of love that we have received from God that we give away. To receive that kind of love and give it away is full of joy that has power to banish unhappiness.

Father, we are too prone to use a measuring stick to give others love that You never used on us. Forgive us!

## 4-18
### Church Attendance

Attending church does not have the priority with many believers that it should have. The numbers show an alarming trend of neglecting the assembly of believers. Does it matter? Jesus said, "Where two or three are gathered together in My name, I am there in the midst of them" (Matthew 18:20 NKJV). That's why it matters! Our privatization of spirituality is robbing us and leaves us spiritual paupers. We need the assembly of believers because Jesus shows up there. Thomas found that to be true the hard way.

But Thomas, one of the twelve, called Didymus, was not with them when Jesus came. So the other disciples were saying to him, "We have seen the Lord!" But he said to them, "Unless I see in His hands the imprint of the nails, and put my finger into the place of the nails, and put my hand into His side, I will not believe." John 20:24-25 (NASB)

## 4-19
### Love Expels Sin
You do not break the cycles of sin in your life by repeating, "I will not do that". Saying it does not stop it; it only keeps the sin at the forefront of your mind. The answer to sin must be more than, "Just say no!" The only way we can expel sin from our lives is by loving God with our whole being and our neighbor as ourself. The absence of this kind of love is a highway for all manner of sins to take root in our lives. Until we love the good more, we can never rid ourselves of the evil.

"Above all, keep fervent in your love for one another, because love covers a multitude of sins." 1 Peter 4:8 (NASB)


## 4-20
### Completing Our Conversion
Prayer is devoting time to the completion of our own conversion. It is the communication with God that makes us grow; it is the communion that forms us. Completing our conversion is the work of our sanctification. God is in the middle of our transformation when we surrender, trust and obey. Prayer is where we settle all of the issues related to our completion. It is where we advance or where we fall back. It is where we yield to the Spirit for His work in us.

Father, thank You for patiently working in our lives to shape and form us. Grant us grace for this transforming process. Amen!


## 4-21
### The Inner You
The heart is the inner person that we are and that we are becoming. The heart is the unvarnished truth of who I am with all of my secrets. The great work of our lives is done at the level of the heart. It is there that we have a desperate need for authenticity. We can search our own heart by searching the heart of God; that is where we are exposed. This is where I see how unlike the God of love that I really am. It is where I ask for a deeper cleansing.

Father, may we gaze long and hard at You. May that vision enable us to become more and more like You. Amen.

### 4-22
**Preparation For Going**
Prayer cannot be an escape from our mission of incarnation; it is what empowers us for it. Prayer is a departure from the world so that we can reenter it with poise and power. It is the place of the renewal of mission. To get along with Jesus is to feel His heart and see His desires for us and the world. Without this we can not fulfill our mission.

Father, enable us to go deeper in You so we can be renewed for the work to which You have called us. Amen

### 4-23
**No Shortcuts**
There are no shortcuts in the spiritual life. There are no tricks of the trade. All that we think we know must become a humble unknowing before we can advance spiritually. We would all like to be more than a novice, more than a rookie, but we are not. There are no big leagues, only minors. We are children. The kingdom is made up of such. Seek no formulas; only seek Him. Seek Him for who He is and not what you want Him to give you.

Father, we come to You as Your child; teach us Your way moment by moment. Amen!

### 4-24
**Rediscover God's Presence**
It is not easy to feel all alone. We have all experienced it at one time or another. You may be living it now. Give a full hearing to the promise: "I will never leave you nor forsake you" (Deuteronomy 31:6, Joshua 1:5, Hebrews 13:5). Jesus put new substance into that OT promise when He said, "I will not leave you as orphans; I will come to you" (John 14:18 ESV). He was speaking of the coming Spirit, the Spirit of Christ Himself. We need to rediscover the Presence with us by focus and conversation with the Presence. He is not an imaginary companion; He is more real than any reality in the universe. He is very near.

**4-25**
**The Way To The Father**
"Jesus is the only Way" is not for in-your-face attacks disguised as evangelism. It was given to Christ's own followers to remind them that they were to walk Jesus as the Road to the Father. It means that we are to seriously follow Christ as the Way to get there. It is more than a profession of faith; this journey to the Father is a way of life, a way of living every moment. When we are walking like Jesus, people will start seeing the Way to the Father.

"Jesus said to him, 'I am the way, and the truth, and the life. No one comes to the Father except through me. If you had known me, you would have known my Father also. From now on you do know him and have seen him.' Philip said to him, 'Lord, show us the Father, and it is enough for us.' Jesus said to him, 'Have I been with you so long, and you still do not know me, Philip? Whoever has seen me has seen the Father. How can you say, 'Show us the Father?'" John 14:6-9 (ESV)

**4-26**
**Social Life**
Social life can be a barrier to true spirituality or a place to live it. To be with God prepares us to be with people. We were meant to bring the life of God to all with whom we come in contact. Loving our neighbor as ourself comes from loving God with our whole being. Our relationship with God our Father is the foundation of our relationship with His other children. Something is missing in all social relationships when we have no vital relationship with God.

Father, thank You for sharing Your life with us so that we can share Your life with all who are in our network. Amen!

**4-27**
**Resting In Faith**
Think of prayer as not finding God, but of learning to rest in God. In this place we can pray without a multitude of words. From this place we can listen to what is on God's mind and heart as we share our mind and heart. Listening is the other half of the conversation, which we sometimes rudely forget. Leaning on God is called trust; resting in God is called faith. This resting in faith is what keeps our vessel aright in the storm and brings us to our haven of rest.

"Rest in the LORD and wait patiently for Him." Psalm 37:7a

## 4-28
### The Fear Of Man
"The LORD is on my side; I will not fear. What can man do to me? (Psalm 118:6, Hebrews 13:6). The fear of the opinions of others can cause us to waver in our commitment to truth. The fear of man distorts justice (Deuteronomy 1:17).
There is a difference in respecting another and fearing another. When we hold God in the place of holy awe and tremble before Him, we can never tremble before a mere man. When we are more concerned about what God knows and thinks about us than man, we will never crumble before opinion polls. When we hold Him high and lifted up, we will never go chasing after the celebrities of pop culture.

"The fear of man lays a snare, but whoever trusts in the LORD is safe." Proverbs 29:25 (ESV)


## 4-29
### The Reason For Unity
In the selection of the 12 disciples one might ask the question, "Can these 12 people even get along with each other? Can a Zealot even be in the same room with a tax collector? Would the hot tempers of the Sons of Thunder, James and John not create ongoing problems? Mix all of these with Thomas, and a bunch of rugged fishermen, and see what will happen. What held them together? Jesus! What did they have in common? Jesus! Who sent them out to change the world? Jesus! If they had not been disciples, they would not have even liked each other. Jesus changed that. When we have Jesus as our common meeting place, differences can be set aside for Him and our common Father.

"Now it came to pass in those days that He went out to the mountain to pray, and continued all night in prayer to God. And when it was day, He called His disciples to Himself; and from them He chose twelve whom He also named apostles". Luke 6:12-13 (NKJV)

## 4-30
### Come To My Aid
"Oh God, come to my aid" was a prayer of the early desert fathers. It was a prayer repeated in times of distress. It is a prayer that we have all prayed in one form or another. It is an appropriate prayer to our Father. He loves us. He cares. He wants to work in our lives for our growth and development. He wants to shape us in Christlike character. He often helps us while we are helping others. He comes to our aid as we come to the aid of His other children. He has some truly amazing and surprising ways of answering our prayers.


## 5-1
### The Irrepressible Message
Jesus is alive. Death is defeated. The world commands us to keep quiet and let everyone enjoy their own private spirituality. The early disciples said, "We cannot stop speaking about what we have seen and heard." They could not keep quiet about the Resurrected One; God's long promised messiah had arrived. He came out of the grave with a body like none had ever seen; the promised future had arrived. They went out to turn the world upside down, never wavering, never silent, even paying with their own lives. They were bearers of an irrepressible message. May this message grip us like it gripped them.

"And when they had summoned them, they commanded them not to speak or teach at all in the name of Jesus. But Peter and John answered and said to them, "Whether it is right in the sight of God to give heed to you rather than to God, you be the judge; for we cannot stop speaking about what we have seen and heard." Acts 4:18-20 (NASB)


## 5-2
### Christlikeness In The OT (1)
The Arameans were making war with Israel, by a miracle of blindness Elisha "captured" them and led them to the king, who wanted to kill his enemies (2 Kings 6:1-23). Elisha would not permit it. Instead he told the king to give his enemies a great feast, and it changed the relationship of two nations. There were many examples of killing your enemies in the OT, but here a Christlike reaction was posed that changed everything. The story was, don't kill your enemies, serve them and feed them and make them your friends. This was more

than diplomacy this is radical love that was revolutionary. This was Christlike peacemaking.

"When the king of Israel saw them, he asked Elisha, 'Shall I kill them, my father? Shall I kill them?' 'Do not kill them,' he answered. 'Would you kill men you have captured with your own sword or bow? Set food and water before them so that they may eat and drink and then go back to their master.' So he prepared a great feast for them, and after they had finished eating and drinking, he sent them away, and they returned to their master. So the bands from Aram stopped raiding Israel's territory" 2 Kings 6:21-23 (NIV). "Never avenge yourselves...To the contrary, "if your enemy is hungry, feed him; if he is thirsty, give him something to drink; for by so doing you will heap burning coals on his head." Do not be overcome by evil, but overcome evil with good." Romans 12:19-21 (ESV)

**5-3**
**Christlikeness In The OT (2)**
The story of Joseph (Genesis 43-45) is one of the most powerful and moving stories in the OT. Joseph was sorely mistreated by his brothers. Their mistreatment ended in slavery and exile for Joesph, away from homeland and family. He had a chance to retaliate, but did not; instead, he invites all his brothers and their families to Egypt to feed them for the duration of the famine. He used his mistreatment to bring salvation, as did Jesus. He graciously forgives the very ones who sinned against him, as did Jesus.

"Then Joseph said to his brothers, 'Please come closer to me.' And they came closer. And he said, 'I am your brother Joseph, whom you sold into Egypt...You shall live in the land of Goshen, and you shall be near me, you and your children and your children's children and your flocks and your herds and all that you have. There I will also provide for you, for there are still five years of famine to come, and you and your household and all that you have would be impoverished.'...He kissed all his brothers and wept on them, and afterward his brothers talked with him." Genesis 45:4,10-11,15 (NASB)

**5-4**
**Christlikeness In The OT (3)**
Esau had been ill-treated and cheated by Jacob most of his life. Jacob cheated him out of his birthright and his blessing. Esau was so angry that he threatened

to kill him after his father died. The two brothers lived apart and were alienated from youth to adulthood. When the day finally came that Esau could carry out his threat to kill his brother, and he had an army to do so, he relented and forgave. He forgot about having justice, vengeance and retaliation and fell in the arms of his brother with a weeping embrace. On that day he was free from that old bitterness that had crippled his soul. He stumbled onto Christlikeness.

"And Jacob lifted up his eyes, and looked, and, behold, Esau came, and with him four hundred men. And he divided the children unto Leah, and unto Rachel, and unto the two handmaids. And he put the handmaids and their children foremost, and Leah and her children after, and Rachel and Joseph hindermost. And he passed over before them, and bowed himself to the ground seven times, until he came near to his brother. And Esau ran to meet him, and embraced him, and fell on his neck, and kissed him: and they wept." Genesis 33:1-4 (KJV)

**5-5**
**Christlikeness In The OT (4)**
"If your enemy is hungry feed him, and if he is thirsty give him something to drink." (Proverbs 20:21 later quoted in Romans 12:20). The book of Leviticus (19:18) said, "Love your neighbor," and many assumed that meant, "Hate your enemy." The above proverb was a denial of that assumption. Paul sees the reason behind this command to give food and water to your enemy and adds his commentary: "Do not be overcome by evil, but overcome evil with good" (Romans 12:21). The evil actions of enemies can only be overcome if we refuse retaliation and give good in return for evil. That is a much better way to live than to live with anger, resentment and hatred. Follow this way of Christ, so well stated in an OT proverb.

**5-6**
**Not My Will**
We as Christians often speak of a surrendered will. We see this as the foundational decision on which to build a life of holiness. Yet we also believe that we are to choose, or will the good. These two ideas are not mutually exclusive. The answer is: to will what God wills. It is expressed by Jesus in the garden. "Father, if you are willing, remove this cup from me. Nevertheless, not my will, but yours, be done" (Luke 22:42 ESV).

## 5-7
### Repairing God-torn Barriers
At the moment of Jesus' death the 90 ft. tall veil in the temple was split from top to bottom, opening the way into the Most Holy Place. The event would likely have been witnessed at that hour by a priest burning incense. For Christians, a new and Living Way is opened through Christ the New Temple, no more animal sacrifices; the approach to God has forever changed by our Mediator. Yet the temple would continue to function for 35 plus years until 70 A.D. This meant that priests would need to repair this thick massive curtain, priests no longer serving God, but working against Him. How do you close what God has opened? Why do we resort to finding other ways around God's way? Self-serving institutions and people will always try! Christ also brought down the barriers between Jew and Gentile, male and female, and all ethnic and racial groups. Repairing God-torn barriers is degenerate and diabolical work. Christ, via the cross, has opened the door, "the open door which no one can shut" (Revelation 3:8).

"And Jesus cried out again with a loud voice, and yielded up His spirit. And behold, the veil of the temple was torn in two from top to bottom" (Matthew 27:50-51a(NIV)

## 5-8
### Beyond Beautiful Thoughts
Our devotional life must move beyond mere sentimentality and beautiful thoughts. This can mask itself as true spirituality. Human words can be a beautiful thing to consider. Spirituality is rooted in a commitment to our Creator God. It is a blend of awe and worship, along with faith and trust. It is an inner knowing of One who is the Essence for which our souls long. Poetry, prose and oratory can point to Him, but we know that our relationship to Him is beyond all of these beautiful thoughts.

"My people come to you, as they usually do, and sit before you to listen to your words, but they do not put them into practice. With their mouths they express devotion, but their hearts are greedy for unjust gain. Indeed, to them you are nothing more than one who sings love songs with a beautiful voice and plays an instrument well, for they hear your words but do not put them into practice."
Ezekiel 33:31-32 (NIV)

## 5-9
## A Living Faith
Our faith is to be a living faith expressed as an ongoing relationship with our Lord. It is too easy to rest in the platitudes of the past generation. Religious groups have an agreed-on language that marks their tribe. Sadly, learning this language is often mistaken for discipleship. Being a disciple of Jesus is more than the language we might use to describe it. It is a present trust and ongoing confidence in our risen Lord. Because He lives, our faith is infused with His life in a vital living hope.

"Blessed be the God and Father of our Lord Jesus Christ! According to his great mercy, he has caused us to be born again to a living hope through the resurrection of Jesus Christ from the dead." 1 Peter 1:3 (ESV)

## 5-10
## Unrelenting Trouble
Troubles can hit us like a storm whose relentless winds just keep pounding. We hunker down, praying desperate prayers that it will soon pass. These times become moments when faith is demonstrated by our grip on the One to whom we say, "I will not let You go." But remember, He has you in the grip of His grace, cradled in His arms, like a mother who pulls a crying child close. He is with you in all of your troubles. He is with you in all of your storms. He will not forget.

"Can a mother forget the baby at her breast and have no compassion on the child she has borne? Though she may forget, I will not forget you!" Isaiah 49:15 (NIV)

## 5-11
## Humility And Spiritual Warfare
"Humble yourselves...your adversary is seeking to devour you" (I Peter 5:6, 8). Included in this exhortation is to "cast your anxieties on Him...your adversary is seeking to devour you" (v. 7-8). Is not this warning us that pride and anxiety is a crack in the door through which the devil can gain a foothold in our lives. Humility and total trust of our situation to the Lord is a way to gain victory over the enemy of our soul.

"Humble yourselves, therefore, under the mighty hand of God so that at the proper time he may exalt you, casting all your anxieties on him, because he cares for you. Be sober-minded; be watchful. Your adversary the devil prowls around like a roaring lion, seeking someone to devour." 1 Peter 5:6-8 (ESV)

### 5-12
### Gospel Power

There is power in the Christ of the cross to redeem and change lives. To neglect the message of the cross is to empty our preaching and witnessing of power to actually transform hearers. Good advice, self-help talks, and pulpit psychology will not serve to break the true chains that hold the lost. The gospel of the cross "is the power of God for salvation to everyone who has faith, to the Jew first and also to the Greek" (Romans 1:16 NRSV). Holy Spirit power is joined with the message of the cross.

"When I came to you, brothers and sisters, I did not come proclaiming the mystery of God to you in lofty words or wisdom. For I decided to know nothing among you except Jesus Christ, and him crucified." 1 Corinthians 2:1-2 (NRSV)

### 5-13
### God Makes Himself Known

The energy that created and maintains creation is a witness to the God from which it proceeds. The acts of God in the lives of His people declare Him. Jesus is the supreme revelation of God, validated by His resurrection. God reveals Himself by His Spirit in prevenient grace. All of these overtures of grace do not predestine nor force belief. They are an invitation to embrace the One who has already embraced us.

"Simon Peter answered, 'You are the Messiah, the Son of the living God.' And Jesus answered him, 'Blessed are you, Simon son of Jonah! For flesh and blood has not revealed this to you, but my Father in heaven.'" Matthew 16:16-17 (NRSV)

### 5-14
### Closed In

There is nothing sadder than a soul closed in on itself. What is going on inside eclipses the beauty of the surrounding horizon; the heart has lost its wonder and nothing holds it in awe. It can barely see the suffering of the world around it, since it is thinking of its own pain. God is not closed in on Himself, for He is ever loving, serving and sustaining His creation. The way out of this dark tunnel is to open yourself to the ever-flowing grace of our Lord; it declares we are loved and have value. From that reality, celebrate the souls around you.

"Why are you in despair, O my soul? And why have you become disturbed within me? Hope in God, for I shall again praise Him For the help of His presence." Psalm 42:5 (NASB)

## 5-15
### The Spirit Points To Jesus
The Spirit in us points to Jesus. Both Simeon and Ana had the Spirit speak through them about the infant Jesus (Luke 2:25-37). Jesus said, "When He the Spirit of Truth comes,...He will glorify me" (John 16:13-14). The power of the Spirit has been used in self-serving ways by charlatans and money grabbers. The true power of the Spirit is given to point to Jesus in our witness (Acts 1:8). The filling of the Spirit is not about us, but about Jesus. The test of the fullness of the Spirit is whether we are centered in Christ.

## 5-16
### A Benediction For The Suffering
"And the God of all grace, who called you to his eternal glory in Christ, after you have suffered a little while, will himself restore you and make you strong, firm and steadfast. To him be the power for ever and ever. Amen" (1 Peter 5:10-11 NIV). Suffering is temporary in the grand scheme of things. While we are suffering we need to know that we are sustained by "the God of all grace". He gives grace to sustain us in the midst of suffering, to make us strong, and unwavering in faith. This beautiful benediction is given to reassure that God is doing something in us in the midst of our suffering. To God be the glory! Amen!

## 5-17
### Mocking The Kingdom
The King of the Jews was mocked with a robe, a crown of thorns, and a stick for a scepter. This was intended to be mockery of His "kingdom". The mockery was meant to say that His kingdom was not to be taken seriously. The disciples

thought He came to develop a strong military to overthrow their enemies. Jesus rejected outrightly being that kind of Messiah. Even today some of His followers do not take His kingdom seriously; it is thought not to be realistic in a world where power wins. Ignoring it has the same outcome as mocking it; His kingship and kingdom is still rejected.

"They stripped him and put a scarlet robe on him, and after twisting some thorns into a crown, they put it on his head. They put a reed in his right hand and knelt before him and mocked him, saying, 'Hail, King of the Jews!'" Matthew 27:28-29 (NRSV)

## 5-18
### Doing Kingdom Work
Every Sunday the *insiders* give lip service to working in the vineyard. They have learned all the right things to say. They say, "We will work", yet, when the work presents itself to them they do not do it. There are a whole cadre of *outsiders* who said no to doing the work of the kingdom, but find themselves doing the good that they said they would not do. These *outsiders* are helping the weak, healing the hurting, welcoming the stranger, etc., when the *insiders* are doing their own thing. These did not say the right thing, but they did the right thing, i.e. the Kingdom thing.

"What do you think? A man had two sons; he went to the first and said, 'Son, go and work in the vineyard today.' He answered, 'I will not'; but later he changed his mind and went. The father went to the second and said the same; and he answered, 'I go, sir'; but he did not go. Which of the two did the will of his father?" They said, "The first." Jesus said to them, "Truly I tell you, the tax collectors and the prostitutes are going into the kingdom of God ahead of you. (Matthew 21:28-31 NRSV)

## 5-19
### God Speaks
Our God is a speaking God. "He made known his ways unto Moses, his acts unto the children of Israel" Psalm 103:7. He who spoke in times past by prophets has now spoken finally and authoritatively through His Son (Hebrews 1:1-4). The Bible is a grand story that culminates with the arrival of the Son, the establishment of His Kingdom, and the summing up of all things in heaven and

earth through Him. All things were "created by Him and for Him" (Colossians 1:15-16). The whole Bible moves toward Him. In our reading of the holy writings we must not get sidetracked into trivia and miss Him. He is the Main Thing. Get to know Him better. Live with Him, and you will hear the speaking God.

## 5-20
### Overcoming Temptation
The statement made about Jesus, "He was without sin," is about more than Jesus' preparation as the unblemished sacrifice; it is also a pattern of victory He has laid down for us as our example. Christ demonstrated in His temptations that we do not need to comply with the enemy of our souls. Satan's temptations can and should be resisted. He finally taught us how to avoid sin by loving God with our whole being and our neighbor as ourselves. He said that this summarized all the commands of the whole Bible. He is teaching us that, at its heart, sin is a failure to love. When we love, it covers a multitude of sins by avoiding them. He said more than once to those He healed, "Go, and sin no more." To expect defeat is to ensure it. Follow the victory of Christ's example in regard to temptation. The whole Bible was written "so that you may not sin"(1 John 2:1), but if we do sin, we go to our Advocate, praying to never repeat that sin again.

## 5-21
### "But I Say To You"
Jesus said, "You have heard it was said...but I say to you." In this statement, the OT is put in its place. It shows that one era has passed, and the promised "age to come" has arrived. The NT now becomes our pattern for living. So many are stuck here: "You have heard it said." They can quote it accurately. The OT version of the Ten Commandments and all the other commandments are their chapter and verse. That's where they live. That's what they know. They have never graduated to this: "But I say to you." They have never allowed His version of the commandments to dig them up and replant them (Matthew 5-7). They are stuck in a self-righteous moralism that can never give them the freedom found in living out the teachings of Jesus. They have never truly heard the Sermon on the Mount, because they are camping at Mount Sinai. Make it your goal to really hear Rabbi Jesus' words, "But I say to you," and live in His age to come.

## 5-22
### Get The Color Right
You thought it was one color, but you got it into the sunlight and found out that it was different than you thought. That is the way it is when we bring ourselves to the fullness of the light found in Jesus, the Light of the world. "Every way of a man is right in his own eyes, But the LORD weighs the hearts" (Proverbs 21:2 NKJV). I do not want to be right only in my own eyes. I need the Light of God on all of my thoughts, words and actions, or I will never see the colors clearly.

## 5-23
### Changing Your Future
You cannot change your past, but you can change your future. The past will never let us change it. We can deny it or misrepresent it, but it is what it is. What we can do is learn from it and release it for a new future. We can by faith and obedience today do the things that will change all our tomorrows, and thus someday, give us a better past. Built into creation are opportunities to start over. Four seasons give us another chance to plant and harvest. Day ends with night, and a new day comes with new potential. A new future is not possible without evaluating where we are, prayerful resolve, and changing behaviors to get us there. The Lord is present in our lives to give us grace at every point in the process of change toward our maturity.

Father, we are so glad that you are the One Who gives us chances for a new start. Amen!

## 5-24
### Good And Evil
God creates the good; evil is nothing but the distortion of the good. Evil must hide behind the good to make itself acceptable. This is why a wolf must wear sheep's clothing. Evil's promises wear the mask of the promises of God, but it is another disguise. Going the route of evil to get to what it promises dehumanizes us. It leaves us deceived and empty. It does not stop there. The evil ends in death. The good ends in life.

"Abhor what is evil. Cling to what is good." Romans 12:9 (NKJV)

## 5-25
### Silent Before Him

God is a complex Being. He is in a category all by Himself; angels, humans and other heavenly creatures are millions of light years in distance from His magnificence. He is far grander than we can ever begin to grasp. God knows the intricate complexities of everything in the universe: everything in the human body, every animal, fish and bird, every particle, cell and atom, all waves and rays, energy, time and matter, and a million other things that should be on this list. Even so, He is patient with those who oversimplify His Person and His marvelous creation, and who actually do so to preserve their theology, science, politics, religion, and their corner on knowledge, while blinded by their own blissful certainty. Such persons want no mystery, simply because they can't control it; they have no god greater than themselves and seem oblivious to their plight.

Father, forgive us when we think we have to explain everything. May we be among those who sit in silence and awe before You, knowing that a statement could ruin everything. May we learn how to worship with wonder, praise and speechless adoration!

## 5-26
### Pray Always

It is easier to talk about prayer than to pray. It is easier to solicit prayer for the requests we pass on than to be a person of prayer ourselves. Prayer requires that we engage our spirit with the Spirit of our Father. We approach Him with awe for the King and with affection for our Father. We bow before Him making our request known. We intercede with more than passing thoughts. We talk to Him; we silently listen to Him. Worship is being in the presence of God to praise Him. Intercession is being in the presence of God on behalf of another. Prayer is being in the presence of God for real conversation.

"Then Jesus told his disciples a parable to show them that they should always pray and not give up." Luke 18:1 (NIV)

## 5-27
### Our Baggage

We all are marked by the genetics of our ancestors. We have been shaped by positive and negative forces. We have made choices that have gone into making us who we are. We may have emotional scars and bitter memories. We have our joys mixed with our sorrows. We have personality traits that may or may not serve us well. This is our baggage. All of us have it. We need to be as patient with other folks' baggage as we want them to be with ours. That is the patience that works by love.

"Owe no one anything, except to love each other, for the one who loves another has fulfilled the law." Romans 13:8 (ESV)

**5-28**
**The Aspects Of Maturity**
We tend to think mostly of becoming mature in regard to sanctification's growth process. That is true. That is the broad brush. But I have been thinking about other aspects of maturity. There is the maturity of faith, which is to trust Him at all times without hesitancy or faltering. There is the maturity of patience, which knows how to keep anger away. There is the maturity of perseverance, which keeps pressing forward to the goal. There is the maturity of joy, which rejoices in the right things. There is the maturity of gentleness, which needs not repress some contrary thought. There is the maturity of emotions, when we do not allow emotions to push us to places we have learned not to go. There is the maturity of meekness and humility where wrongful pride has died. We need the Spirit to help us to develop these and many other aspects of maturity.

**5-29**
**Get Up! Keep Running!**
Just because we are down does not mean we are out. Just because we stumble does not mean we must get out of the race. Get back up, and keep going. Even though someone deliberately tripped us does not mean that we retreat to the bench. Keep running, even when your muscles and joints protest. Keep running, looking to Jesus (Hebrews 12:1-2). He is our Example. He is our Coach. He is the Prize. In Him all good things await us. Determine to finish the race. Never give up!

"Therefore lift your drooping hands and strengthen your weak knees, and make straight paths for your feet, so that what is lame may not be put out of joint but rather be healed. Strive for peace with everyone, and for the holiness without which no one will see the Lord. See to it that no one fails to obtain the grace of God." Hebrews 12:12-15a (ESV)

## 5-30
### Genuinely Love
"I love you" can come from a heart that really does. Sometimes the words can come from those who really do not. "Don't just pretend to love others. Really love them. Hate what is wrong. Hold tight to what is good. Love each other with genuine affection, and take delight in honoring each other" (Romans 12:9-10, NLT). Love shows itself in more than affection; it shows itself with honor and respect. This means that we revere those we love. We give them a special places in our thoughts, and then in how we treat them.

## 5-31
### Earnest Asking
At the top of our asking in prayer is asking for the Holy Spirit. We are in constant need of being filled afresh and anew with the Spirit. Our prayer life can degenerate into asking for things. He is to be at the top of our asking, seeking and knocking. The idea conveyed in Luke 11 is that this is not casual asking but it is serious-soul-hunger asking, a deep inner yearning. It's like a deer panting for the water brooks (Psalm 42:1-2). T.W. Willingham once said, "It is unthinkable to me that God would give His Spirit to anyone that did not want the Spirit more than they wanted a new car or a new television set."

"So I say to you: Ask and it will be given to you; seek and you will find; knock and the door will be opened to you. For everyone who asks receives; he who seeks finds; and to him who knocks, the door will be opened. Which of you fathers, if your son asks for a fish, will give him a snake instead? Or if he asks for an egg, will give him a scorpion? If you then, though you are evil, know how to give good gifts to your children, how much more will your Father in heaven give the Holy Spirit to those who ask him!" Luke 11:9-13 (NIV)

## 6-1
### Seek Harmony And Peace
The Bible has much more to say about how humans relate to each other than we have yet heard. "Live in harmony with each other. Don't be too proud to enjoy

the company of ordinary people. And don't think you know it all! Never pay back evil with more evil. Do things in such a way that everyone can see you are honorable. Do all that you can to live in peace with everyone" (Romans 12:16-18, NLT). Reread and soak in these words. Do these things in all of your relationships. Avoid those ingrained habits that hinder this. This kind of living will change you, as well as the world around you for the better.

## 6-2
### Deeper! Deeper!
We may have become a generation of Christians who are a mile wide and an inch deep. We have ceased to think deeply about the grand truths of Christianity. We need to think about how Trinity, incarnation, atonement, and other Christian truths fit together as part of a beautiful story. Our shallowness does not serve us well in desert places. We become deep by tapping into the deep wells of Truth, the Spirit and the Word. We avoid shallowness by exploring the grand story of redemption beyond cliches that have long since lost their meaning. To grow deeper is far more than academic; it must be experiential in our relationship with our Father. Growing knowledge should always be paired with growing faith.

"And we know that the Son of God has come and has given us understanding so that we may know him who is true; and we are in him who is true, in his Son Jesus Christ. He is the true God and eternal life." 1 John 5:20 (NRSV)

## 6-3
### Acting On God's Nature
The way believers are to act and react in every area of their lives should be based on the nature of God. What is the nature of God? What is God like? Look at Jesus! We see God in the face of Jesus. We know what He is like because we have seen Jesus. Jesus is the benchmark we come back to for the way we live our lives. Acting on God's nature, as it is revealed in Christ, is the goal of our formation. To say it another way, we are to live out the Nature of our Father. Let His DNA shine through you.

"So Jesus said to them, 'Truly, truly, I say to you, the Son can do nothing of his own accord, but only what he sees the Father doing. For whatever the Father does, that the Son does likewise.'" John 5:19 (ESV)

## 6-4
### Balanced Praying
We pray often for ourselves and the needs of those we love. My prayers for all of my needs should be balanced by prayers for all of your needs. My prayers for my children and grandchildren need to be balanced with praying for your children and grandchildren. Intercession for others keeps my prayer life from being entirely self-centered. Pray for the lost, the sick, the hungry, the abandoned, the forgotten, the imprisoned, the lonely, the widow, the orphan, the trafficked child, and all the hurting ones around us that we have not yet even seen.

"With all prayer and petition pray at all times in the Spirit, and with this in view, be on the alert with all perseverance and petition for all the saints." Ephesians 6:18 (NASB)

## 6-5
### Neglect Not The Widow
"The widow who is really in need and left all alone puts her hope in God and continues night and day to pray and to ask God for help" (1 Timothy 5:5 NIV). You do not read far in the Old or New Testament without seeing that God is really concerned about widows. One of the first things the NT church did was to organize itself to take care of them. The widowed not only deal with grief and loneliness, but they deal with a whole set of problems just to survive. They are quickly forgotten. They are invisible in a room. They suffer in silence. List all the ones you know. Use your sanctified imagination to reach out to them in small and large ways.

"Pure and undefiled religion in the sight of our God and Father is this: to visit orphans and widows in their distress, and to keep oneself unstained by the world." James 1:27 (NASB)

## 6-6
### Incomplete Conversions
I believe in the new birth. I believe in a moment of change. But I also know that all the changing that needs to happen in our lives does not happen in that first moment. We have been converted, and we are being converted. Grace is drawing us to change things in our life, break old habits, and add some new ones. Ongoing repentance is the path to that. Sanctification is the process.

Ways of thinking are deeply entrenched as was the racism of Peter in Galatians 2:11ff. His behavior needed to be converted to Christian teaching. He believed it but was not yet practicing it.

Lord, I am so thankful that You are at work in my life, still shaping, still changing. Keep sanctifying me by Your truth for Your word is truth. Help me to become what You dream for me, oh Father.

## 6-7
### Un-controlling Love

Believing that God controls every decision and action of humankind, both good and evil, is so unlike the One God revealed in Trinity. God does not control; He loves. The Father, Son and Spirit (One God) exists in a community of unbroken love. Neither controls the Other, Each prefers the Other and testifies of the Other out of self-effacing love. The Son shows us the Father and the Spirit shows us the Son, etc. The spotlight is always turned on the Other. The members of the Trinity do not do selfies. If the goal of the Christian's life is to be restored to divine likeness, then to be like God is to focus in love on others.

"Do nothing out of selfish ambition or vain conceit, but in humility consider others better than yourselves. Each of you should look not only to your own interests, but also to the interests of others" Philippians 2:3-4 (NIV).

## 6-8
### A Daily Mercy

In the hymn, "Come Thou Fount" there is a phrase which says, "Streams of mercy, never ceasing." I am captured by the thought. The Fount produces an unending stream of mercy. Wow! We forget that we need mercy constantly flowing into our lives. We need mercy more than at the time of our conversion; we always need it. We need mercy for our lagging growth, for our mistakes, shortcomings and plain ignorance. Are you not amazed at God's patience with you? Where would we be without it? Lord, have mercy! Lord, have mercy! Lord, have mercy!

"Our eyes look to the LORD our God, until he has mercy upon us. Have mercy upon us, O LORD, have mercy upon us, for we have had more than enough of contempt." Psalm 123:2b-3 (NRSV)

## 6-9
### Coping Skills

Life has a way of testing our strength and challenging our coping skills. One way of coping is to be patient with those who are not coping. Sometimes we have mastered some things with which others may still be struggling. We must understand that they may not be where we are. Let the way we cope with life be a model and guide to them. Let us help them. Put yourself in their place, the place you used to be, the place you were when you were not coping all that well. Give them that mercy.

"Since God chose you to be the holy people he loves, you must clothe yourselves with tenderhearted mercy, kindness, humility, gentleness, and patience. Make allowance for each other's faults, and forgive anyone who offends you. Remember, the Lord forgave you, so you must forgive others." Colossians 3:12-13 (NLT)

## 6-10
### Superstition And 666

The evil is not the number 666, but what it represents. The first readers of Revelation understood its meaning to their present persecution. Multiple scholars remind us that 666 is a code word in OT and NT for the oppressive empire. In the OT the weight of gold that came to Solomon in taxes was 'six hundred sixty-six talents of gold" (2 Chronicles 9:13 NRSV) (I Kings 10:14). The writer of I Kings is telling us something. Solomon's oppressive powers had become like Pharaoh. Pharaoh had made slaves of Israel, and later, by forced labor and power of empire, Solomon again made slaves out of God's people. The Roman empire apparently gave a mark to certify that you had said, "Caesar is Lord," to buy and sell. It was their way of merging nationalism with religion, always a dangerous mix. The sad thing about locking in on the number is that many trust the empire more than God and do not know that they have thus already taken the mark.

Father, may our love for You and Your kingdom be so central that we never let the governments of men consume us and get their mark on us. Amen!

## 6-11
### Idols Of Holy Things
Moses made a serpent of brass at the command of the Lord (Numbers 21:9). People were saved from snake bites by looking to it. However, in time it became a relic to worship. In an odd way, holy things can become central to worship: A church building, prayer, fasting, the Bible, a pastor, a teacher, an institution, etc. Means must not become ends of worship. Nothing must be allowed to turn our eyes from the Lord, not even holy things. "Little children, keep yourselves from idols. Amen." (1 John 5:21)

"He broke in pieces the bronze serpent that Moses had made, for until those days the people of Israel had made offerings to it." 2 Kings 18:4 (ESV)

## 6-12
### As To The Lord
"And whatever you do, do it heartily, as to the Lord and not to men" (Colossians 3:23 NKJV). This Pauline advice to slaves is advice that we could all profit from in our daily lives. We do not always like the tasks that we need to do. Routine can become boring. Some assignments can be drudgery. This verse tells us that if we would do everything we do as if it were direct service to Jesus our Lord, it would change everything. This changes the secular into the sacred; it changes all of life into acts of worship.

## 6-13
### Without Excuse
In some quarters, there is a pessimistic view of ever really living a holy life. What we must understand is that our loving Father has provided everything we need to live holy and godly lives. The cleansing by the Son, the abiding of the Holy Spirit, and the great promises of God's word come together as unfailing resources toward living Christlike/holy lives. This holiness does not originate with us but comes from partaking of the very nature of God. That He would share the precious Essence of who He is with washed sinners truly boggles my mind.

"His divine power has granted to us all things that pertain to life and godliness, through the knowledge of him who called us to his own glory and excellence, by which he has granted to us his precious and very great promises, so that through them you may become partakers of the divine nature, having escaped from the corruption that is in the world because of sinful desire." 2 Peter 1:3-4 (ESV)

## 6-14
### Listening To The Spirit
Truly listening to the Spirit who has come to live inside of us is radically life changing. He will change our praying, what we ask for, what we seek, what we live for, and what we value. People will become more important than things. He will check us when Mammon starts to edge its way into our lives. He will help our character to advance toward Christlike maturity, for without His grace we cannot make advances in our spiritual growth and ultimate formation. Get away from the noise. Quiet your soul. Listen to The Spirit.

"Are your ears awake? Listen. Listen to the Wind Words, the Spirit blowing through the churches." Revelation 3:6 (MSG)

## 6-15
### The Mirage
We are constantly shown images of perfect lives, bodies, jobs, and families. These images are not harmless. They create distress. They create entries to voices in our heads about how everyone else has it so good and we have it so bad. It is really the sin of envy. It is a mirage. It looks like something refreshing from a distance, but when you get close, it goes away. All humans have their flaws, brokenness and problems; they may successfully hide it behind a perfect image. Let the Lord help you deal with the not-so-perfect things in your life. Stop wishing away your problems, seek solutions and start to grow.

"But if you harbor bitter envy and selfish ambition in your hearts, do not boast about it or deny the truth. Such "wisdom" does not come down from heaven but is earthly, unspiritual, of the devil. For where you have envy and selfish ambition, there you find disorder and every evil practice." James 3:14-16 (NIV)

## 6-16
### Recovering Pity
The word pity has fallen out of common use. It means, "feeling of sorrow and compassion caused by the suffering and misfortunes of others." It is an

unexplored dimension of love and compassion for most of us. When we really pause to look, we will see brokenness and hurt in the eyes and faces of our fellow humans. When we have the love of Christ in us, there is something that draws us toward the hurting, not to look down upon them in some condescending way, but something pulls us to them in real healing identification. Our Father has pity for us. Let's practice it for our fellow humans.

"As a father pities his children, So the LORD pities those who fear Him" Psalm 103:13 (NKJV).

## 6-17
### Limit Rejection's Power
Rejection is one of the most difficult things we have to face in life. We may be rejected by a spouse, friend, family or a group. The pain can be overwhelming. Jesus knew rejection at multiple levels. We tend to get stuck there. We focus on and blame the rejector. We can let it consume our thoughts and our days. We must not allow rejection to define who we are. We must determine not to fall in the trap of being the victim. We can use it to identify with our Lord and allow it to be a means of a deeper death to self as well as a means of personal growth in holiness.

"The Son of Man must undergo great suffering, and be rejected by the elders, chief priests, and scribes, and be killed, and on the third day be raised." Luke 9:22 (NRSV)

## 6-18
### Enduring Love
"His steadfast love endures forever" (Psalm 100:5b). God loves us as our faithful Spouse. In sickness and poverty His love endures. When we are at our worst, love is there to help us. When we are at our best, it rejoices with us. His love is steadfast and not fickle, fading or forsaking. He is there with us when no one else is. This love endures; it is patient and persevering. It overcomes all that would frustrate it.

Father, thank You for your enduring love for us, your frail children.

## 6-19
### Death And Life
All plants and animals are dependent on the life that has gone before it. Dead organic matter feeds plants, animals and humans. Something dies that other things might live. Is that not one of the messages of the cross? Life begets life. That's the creation story. Is this not the message of the Lord's Supper? The Bread of Heaven has been given for the life of the world.

"This is the bread which came down out of heaven; not as the fathers ate and died; he who eats this bread will live forever." John 6:58 (NASB)

## 6-20
### Everlasting Kingdom
Nebuchadnezzar had a vision of a huge shining statue of a man that was crushed by a stone rolling down a mountain. Daniel interpreted it to be the end of the governments of men and the arrival of the kingdom of God (Daniel 2:ff.). In the vision we see that the governments of men are temporary and the Kingdom of God is permanent. We need that perspective. This will change how we view our nation. It too will become "like the chaff of the summer threshing floor". It will save us a lot of anxiety and keep us away from a lot of false hopes. Cast your lot with King Jesus and His everlasting Kingdom.

"Then the iron, the clay, the bronze, the silver and the gold were broken to pieces at the same time and became like chaff on a threshing floor in the summer. The wind swept them away without leaving a trace. But the rock that struck the statue became a huge mountain and filled the whole earth. ...In the time of those kings, the God of heaven will set up a kingdom that will never be destroyed, nor will it be left to another people. It will crush all those kingdoms and bring them to an end, but it will itself endure forever.     Daniel 2:35a, 44 (NIV)

## 6-21
### Meet My Father
Let me tell you about my Father. He is the Architect of the universe. He hung the stars. He gave us the sun by day and the moon by night. He is the Creator of all there is. He is the One who called Abraham. He is the "I am" revealed to Moses. He is the God and Father of our Lord Jesus Christ. He knows what I need before I ask. He hears private prayers that He answers openly. He

promotes. He rewards. He cares. He listens. He speaks. He gives good things. He gives His Spirit. He sees sparrows. He watches out for the orphans, widows and the poor. He sees me. He is in Heaven. He is as near as His Spirit. He forgives trespasses. He wants to give us the Kingdom. He has pity on His children. He is holy. He is love. He is not against us; He is for us. He is patient, longsuffering and kind. He welcomes the prodigal son and entreats the older son to join the party. He is not willing that any perish. He makes the sun to rise. He holds the world in the palm of His hand. He sends sunshine and rain on the just and the unjust. He hangs the rainbow. He paints the sunset. He lifts the lowly. He brings down the mighty. He is higher than the heavens and nearer than the breath we breathe. He dwells with the lowly and contrite. He draws near to those who draw near to Him. His love is deeper than the sea. His kindness is higher than the sky. The transcendent One is immanent. "His mercy is everlasting. His truth endures through all generations."

### 6-22
**Trespasses**
Jesus taught us to ask, "Forgive us our trespasses as we forgive those who trespass against us." Trespasses are when you have crossed a line and go where you should not have gone. It is to go from Eden's bounty over to forbidden fruit. It is to try to be your own god. It is to go against love. All of us, at one time or another have crossed the trespass line. We are to look for more than forgiveness; we are to learn from our sins and failure to live a life in harmony with what the Father expects of us. Wanting to please the Father is a great motive to repeatedly getting it right.

### 6-23
**Elusive Happiness And Joy**
Happiness is so elusive to many people who don't seem to have a clue as to why. Failure to forgive is the thief of happiness and joy. Its cousin, resentment, does its mischief. Pride and arrogance are malignant to the soul. Cutting sarcasm is acid to one's own spirit. Forbidden fruit promises happiness but brings shame. Material things portend happiness but can't deliver. Pleasure pretends to be it. The positive ingredients of happiness are rejoicing in the Lord, complete trust, gratitude, obedience, humility, purity, absolute surrender, the pursuit of holiness and loving God and actually loving your fellow humans.

Father, Your commandments are not grievous. You have given us the path to joy in Your Word. You have taught us that the secret of joy is loving You and serving our neighbor. Holy Spirit, warn us of the detours to this path. Amen!

## 6-24
### Heart Music
Paul's alternative to being drunk with wine is "Singing psalms and hymns and spiritual songs among yourselves, and making music to the Lord in your hearts." The greatness of our God has called out songs from the hearts of God's people down through the ages. Good theology is essential for sound doctrine, but a song is essential for worship. We need to soar in song. Let your spirit be inspired by His Spirit to sing. Your soul needs it.

"Don't be drunk with wine, because that will ruin your life. Instead, be filled with the Holy Spirit, singing psalms and hymns and spiritual songs among yourselves, and making music to the Lord in your hearts. And give thanks for everything to God the Father in the name of our Lord Jesus Christ." Ephesians 5:18-20 (NLT)

## 6-25
### The Kingdom Way
Jesus' teaching on the Kingdom of God is directing us in how we are to be and act in the world. The Kingdom way is the Christian way. It is the Government we live under and the values we espouse. Citizens of the Kingdom cannot glorify another way of living in the world. It calls into question whether or not we truly believe that the Kingdom way is the superior way of living in the world.

"Jesus answered, 'My kingdom is not from this world. If my kingdom were from this world, my followers would be fighting to keep me from being handed over to the Jews. But as it is, my kingdom is not from here.'" John 18:36 (NRSV)

## 6-26
### Untangling Thoughts
The human mind constantly works to form thoughts in orderly and coherent ways. It is not always an easy path. Sometimes we do not think clearly. The Word of God is the way that our thoughts can become untangled. We really do need the teaching of holy scripture. We need the Word of God to correct our

thinking and to reprove our behavior. Untangling our thoughts is the first step in getting our lives untangled.

"All Scripture is inspired by God and profitable for teaching, for reproof, for correction, for training in righteousness; so that the man of God may be adequate, equipped for every good work" 2 Timothy 3:16-17 (NASB).

## 6-27
### Soul Rest
Jesus promised that His yoke would bring rest to the soul (Matthew 11:29). The legalism of the Pharisees had become a yoke for the people that was unbearable. Religion that is all about rules gets pretty heavy real soon. Some thought that the more sacrifices one makes the more pleased God is. Micah's response to those who depended on multiplying sacrifices pointed to a simple way. "He has told you, O man, what is good; and what does the LORD require of you but to do justice, and to love kindness, and to walk humbly with your God?" (Micah 6:8 ESV). If your religion has become a grievous burden, trade it in for a Jesus yoke.

## 6-28
### Something Great
Most of us think we need to do something great for our great God. Certainly He deserves more than we can ever give Him. Sometimes pride may be the driving motive for that. The longer I live, the more I realize that the greatest things we can do for God's kingdom work actually started as something very small. A kind word, a shared meal, discipling, a little mentoring, scattering seeds of love, etc., can prove to have an incredible impact. Don't downplay the little things.

Father, thank You for how You use the small things we do for You in ways more significant the we could ever have dreamed. Amen

## 6-29
### Does Jesus Care?
Sometimes you can be at a place in your life when you ask, "Does anybody care?" You may feel that no one is at all interested in that with which you deal. You may even wonder if God cares. Well, He does. The apostles of our Lord

had been with Jesus. They understood that God is not aloof from the needs of His people. They knew Him to be the caring Shepherd. Hear these words, "Casting all your care upon Him, for He cares for you" 1 Peter 5:7 (NKJV).

## 6-30
### Watch Against Idols
The Great Commandment is really a call to get rid of idols. It instructs us to love God with our whole being without dividing that love with another god. "Hear, O Israel! The LORD is our God, the LORD is one! You shall love the LORD your God with all your heart and with all your soul and with all your might." (Deuteronomy 6:4-5 NASB). The thing that always edges God out of the center is love for another god. The sin of idolatry is never far away from any of us. Idolatry is discoverable in what we love, value and serve.

## 7-1
### Unwitting Hypocrisy
It is possible to say all the right things and be something very different from that. This happens when we claim to be believers without being followers, when we profess Christ as Lord and are very much in charge of our own lives, when we claim Christianity without any serious attempts at discipleship, or when we give lip service without honoring from the heart. Such hypocrisy creeps in on us when we no longer allow the Spirit to examine our hearts and motives.

"The lamp of the LORD searches the spirit of a man; it searches out his inmost being." Proverbs 20:27 (NIV)

## 7-2
### Jesus' Hometown
Jesus returned to His hometown after a preaching mission (Mark 6:1). He taught in His home synagogue. The people He grew up with could not accept Him. They said, "Is not this the carpenter, the son of Mary, and brother of James and Joses and Judas and Simon? Are not His sisters here with us?" (Mark 6:3). They were offended by Him and they rejected Him and His message. We must understand that our witness will not always be accepted by family and close friends.

## 7-3
### Perfect Submission
Twice, in her song "Blessed Assurance," Fanny Crosby uses the words "Perfect Submission." This is a submission that is full and complete. It is a submission to our Lord with nothing held back. It is to relinquish my claim to myself. It is to abdicate the throne of my heart, enthroning Him as Lord of all. It is victory through surrender. It is entire consecration. There is a stream that flows out of this that does indeed bring blessed assurance. Don't settle for anything less than giving the Lord your all.

Father, teach us the fully joy that comes with perfect submission. Bring us to that place of complete rest in You. Amen.

## 7-4
### Real Freedom
The purpose of our freedom is not to do as we please; it is to finally be able to let God do with us as He pleases. Doing everything you want to do will either keep you in bondage or return you to it. "It was for freedom that Christ set us free; therefore keep standing firm and do not be subject again to a yoke of slavery" (Galatians 5:1 NASB). There is nothing more freeing that doing the will of God. We have to be set free to get there and staying there keeps us free.

## 7-5
### Christ Our Wisdom
The teachings of Jesus contain the greatest wisdom in the universe. In Him we hear one greater than Solomon (Matthew 12:42). He was both the Word and Wisdom incarnate, who was with God and was God (John 1:1). By wisdom He created all things (Proverbs 3:19, Psalm 136:5). His wisdom is behind the intelligent design of the universe. It is His wisdom that gives order to our lives. His message on love and forgiveness contains the wisdom that keeps life from coming unhinged.

"Christ Jesus, who became to us wisdom from God, righteousness and sanctification and redemption" 1 Corinthians 1:30 (ESV).

## 7-6
### Real Wisdom And God
We erroneously think that we can arrive at wisdom apart from God. His wisdom is everywhere in the universe; even wicked men can discover bits of it, though

they may not yet acknowledge God as its source. Non-Christian religions can contain truth, because all truth is God's truth. Wisdom is ultimately derived from the Creator God (Psalm 111:10). Worship taps into the Source of wisdom, moving from knowledge to awe. Wisdom from God is the way of transforming humankind.

"The fear of the LORD is the beginning of wisdom; all who follow his precepts have good understanding. To him belongs eternal praise." Psalm 111:10 (NIV)

## 7-7
### Bountiful Harvest
"The one who sows sparingly will also reap sparingly, and the one who sows bountifully will also reap bountifully" (2 Corinthians 9:6 NRSV). The context of this verse was an offering being received for poor Christians in Jerusalem. However, this agricultural analogy can apply to sowing the seeds of the gospel of the Kingdom. The world is fed simply because seeds multiply. The world needs the Bread of Heaven. Sow it generously, while praying for a bountiful harvest.

"Still other seeds fell on fertile soil, and they produced a crop that was thirty, sixty, and even a hundred times as much as had been planted! Anyone with ears to hear should listen and understand." Matthew 13:8-9 (NLT)

## 7-8
### Toward Maturity
We cannot fix that which God alone can fix. We cannot fix other people, though we keep trying. We cannot control what they do, say or think. We live with the consequences of other's choices and actions. It is not easy and is often devastating. What we can do is pray, not only for the other person, but for our own reactions. Our lives grow toward maturity, not in the perfectly controlled environment of a greenhouse, but in the imperfection of human relationships.

Father, we all want a problem-free life, but we find that it always escapes us. We feel we could grow better if that were the case. You are teaching us another way: growth in the midst of our problems. Father, thanks for being patient with us in these and all things. Amen.

## 7-9
### Offsetting Grace
Grace is given to us in added measure when our problems increase. Paul said, "Where sin abounded, grace did much more abound" (Romans 5:20b KJV). He could also have said, "Where problems multiply, grace multiplies even more." That is what we have all found in our walk with the Lord. We are never left in a situation where there is not enough God and grace to deal with it. Be encouraged. By faith pray for it and appropriate it.

Father, thank You that You give grace that is greater than the problems we encounter. May we believe and know that Your grace is always enough. Amen!


## 7-10
### The Gospel Of The Kingdom
Our problem is that we have divorced the gospel from the NT message of the Kingdom and made it only about personal salvation with a free ticket out of here. The very first message of John the Baptist, of Jesus and the twelve was this:
  "Repent for the Kingdom of Heaven has arrived." It was heard as, "God's promised government is here, and Jesus is the Messiah/King of the Kingdom." The rejected King in the days of Samuel has come down to earth. God has reaffirmed kingship through Messiah's Kingdom. Caesar is no longer Lord, nor Is anyone else. Jesus is Lord! The governments of the earth are to give way to the rule of King Jesus. May this worldview get us off of ever-present side tracks so we can live out this grand truth.

"Thy Kingdom come, Thy will be done, on earth as it is in Heaven…for Thine is the Kingdom, and the power, and the glory for ever." Amen!


## 7-11
### Repentance And The Kingdom
"Repent for the Kingdom of Heaven is at hand", i.e., the long awaited government of God is here. So, folks were baptized in the Jordan while confessing their sins (Mark 1:5). What do sins have to do with the Kingdom? Sins against the covenant drove the nation into exile. The nation was lost. To end exile and to rebuild God's future for all people and ethnic groups required that their lives were realigned with the God of the New Covenant. Further, it meant that whatever their political bents were toward the various party groups (Sadducees, Zealots,

Pharisees, Herodians, etc.), these preferences had to give way by repentance to the new arriving reality of God's government.

## 7-12
### Reaffirming Surrender
In this Christian walk, we discover that some of the things we thought we had surrendered once-and-for-all to the Lord we have actually picked up again. We said we had given up mammon for Him, only to find ourselves again in hasty pursuit of it. Covetousness and greed slipped in the side door. We give up power to find ourselves craving it for ourselves and our tribe. It is not always easy to leave something unconditionally with the Lord. The daily surrender is the test of our initial surrender. We must continually keep Christ as our all-in-all or allow Him to subtly become less.

"Therefore we ought to give the more earnest heed to the things which we have heard, lest at any time we should let them slip." Hebrews 2:1 (KJV)

## 7-13
### Investing In People
We are where we are today largely because of other people. If we stand tall, it is because we are standing on the shoulders of those who went before us. We have nothing that we did not receive. What do you owe to parents, grandparents, teachers, neighbors, pastors, friends, mentors, fellow Christians, and classmates? Is there gratitude in your heart for them? Have you thanked them? Are you investing in others the same way others invested in you? Your devotion to Christ compels you to invest in others. It is time to pay back and pay forward.

"What do you have that you did not receive? And if you received it, why do you boast as if it were not a gift?" 1 Corinthians 4:7b (NRSV).

## 7-14
### All On The Altar
John Henry Sammis wrote this verse in the song, "Trust and Obey". "But we never can prove the delights of His love, until all on the altar we lay; For the favor He shows and the joy He bestows, are for them who will trust and obey." There

is so much wisdom in these words. There is misery in half-hearted commitment. Joy comes when Christ truly has all of us. There is a delight in His love that comes with total sacrifice. There is a deeper intimacy with Him after we cut the cords of other allurements.

"Therefore I urge you, brethren, by the mercies of God, to present your bodies a living and holy sacrifice, acceptable to God, which is your spiritual service of worship." Romans 12:1 (NASB)

## 7-15
### God Gives The Increase
"I have planted, Apollos watered; but God gave the increase. So then neither is he that plants anything, neither he that waters; but God that gives the increase." (1 Corinthians 3:6-7). The sower needs the harvester. and the harvester needs the sower. Both need the waterer. God the Farmer uses all kinds of laborers for the increase. The vineyard and the field are His. It is not ours. Oh, how we need to know and feel that. Oh, what an honor to work with Him in His great field called the world!

## 7-16
### Christ's Return And Purity
The return of Christ has now become associated with speculation. Speculative books and movies have produced lots of fear for people and lots of money for writers. This is not the way it is supposed to be. The hope of Christ's return should motivate us toward purity. The fact of becoming like Him should even now cause us to want to put out of our lives everything that is not like Him. This hope should be moving us toward purity and holiness.

"Dear friends, now we are children of God, and what we will be has not yet been made known. But we know that when he appears, we shall be like him, for we shall see him as he is. Everyone who has this hope in him purifies himself, just as he is pure." 1 John 3:2-3 (NIV)

## 7-17
### The Cross-Way Of Living
The cross is the way we find life. It is counterintuitive. We think life must be found some other way. Our Lord taught us that taking up the cross is the secret;

in losing our life we find it, in dying we live, our resurrection follows our death on the cross. The way of the cross is still foolishness to the world, avoided by professed disciples, shunned by those hungry for position and power, and neglected by those called to proclaim it. Keep trying to find yourself and enjoy the frustration. Discover losing yourself and find eternal joy and eternal life.

"Then Jesus said to His disciples, 'If anyone wishes to come after Me, he must deny himself, and take up his cross and follow Me. For whoever wishes to save his life will lose it; but whoever loses his life for My sake will find it'." Matthew 16:24-25 (NASB)

## 7-18
### Repentance And Self-Examination
There is no transformation or growth without repentance. There is no repentance without self-examination. If you want to grow in the knowledge of our Lord and Savior Jesus Christ, then you need to grow in the knowledge of your own self. When you let Him change you, you will know Him better. The most painful, ongoing thing you and I have to do is to look at our own lives through the lens of the eternal Son. Ironically, we see ourselves in studying Him. When I see Him illumined in the pages of Scripture by the Holy Spirit, my prayer is, "Lord, have mercy on me and remake me in Your likeness."

## 7-19
### Call Fire Down
The Sons of Thunder, James and John, wanted to call fire down on inhospitable Samaria. They wanted to kill them and get them out of the way. They could have cited OT precedence for doing so, but Jesus revealed that this would not be the way His Kingdom citizens would react. This was contrary to the Spirit of Jesus. It indicated some other attitude and spirit at work in His disciples. It still does.

"But He turned and rebuked them, and said, 'You do not know what manner of spirit you are of. For the Son of Man did not come to destroy men's lives but to save them.' And they went to another village.'" Luke 9:55-56 (NKJV)

## 7-20
### Intentional Focus
When Elijah was about to depart this earth, Elisha kept a determined focus on his mentor, Elijah. Three times Elisha said, "As the LORD lives, and as you yourself live, I will not leave you" (2 Kings 2:2, 4, 6). The end result was Elijah's mantle and a double portion of the spirit of Elijah (vv. 9-13) came to rest on Elisha. Intentional focus on our Lord is the way to be filled with the Spirit of our Lord. It is the Spirit of Jesus Himself that we need.

"Elijah said to Elisha, 'Stay here; for the LORD has sent me as far as Bethel.' But Elisha said, 'As the LORD lives, and as you yourself live, I will not leave you.' So they went down to Bethel." 2 Kings 2:2 (NRSV)


## 7-21
### The Healing Kingdom
A detachment of Roman soldiers, along with Jewish police (John 18:3), were sent to apprehend Jesus. In order to defend Jesus, Peter cut off the ear of the servant of the high priest with a sword. Jesus used his miracle powers to restore the ear of the slave. In its day, the kingdom of Rome was a state-of-the-art killing machine. Jesus' Kingdom was different. The Kingdom of Messiah was to be a healing kingdom. Those who are our enemies don't need to be slashed; they need to be healed. We cannot win the world while using or cheering the world's methods.

"Then one of them struck the slave of the high priest and cut off his right ear.
But Jesus said, 'No more of this!' And he touched his ear and healed him." Luke 22:50-51 (NRSV)


## 7-22
### Fellowship Of The Spirit
Twice Paul used the phrase, "fellowship of the Holy Spirit" (2 Corinthians 13:14, Philippians 2:1). The Greek word for fellowship carries with it the ideas of: participation, sharing, communion, and partnership. It is more than sitting down for tea or coffee with Him. It is to join Him in a working relationship in His mission to the world. It is a way to bring the forces of heaven to bear on this earth. We want the Spirit to lead us to persons and places for ministry. Fellowship with the Spirit is foundational to all that we accomplish for God.

## 7-23
### "Busyness"
We can become involved in a kind of "busyness" that keeps us from more important tasks, yes, even in the church. We get preoccupied with the insignificant and miss the significant. Without priorities we will not get the consequential and essential things done. "Busyness" with the minor may make us feel good about our service, while we are neglecting the major. Meeting people needs should have priority over meeting institutional needs. Sitting at the feet of our Rabbi is more important than our daily to-do lists.

"And Jesus answered and said to her, 'Martha, Martha, you are worried and troubled about many things. But one thing is needed, and Mary has chosen that good part, which will not be taken away from her.'" Luke 10:41-42 (NKJV)

## 7-24
### Fresh Language
You know what clichés are, old, tired and trite phrases that no longer communicate to the hearers, nor even to the speakers. There are those who know how to use the accepted phrases of a religious culture in their conversations, testimonies and prayers to gain acceptance among their religious peers. We need something fresh in our language to express to and about our Lord. This shows romance, depth and joy as new treasures of truth are uncovered. Sincere love, genuine integrity and intimate worship with God can free us from the trite, enabling us to taste the real adventure of walking with our Lord, and maintain vitality in the relationship.

Father, forgive us when we say words that have no real meaning to us. May our relationship with You be so fresh and new each day that what we say flows out of a genuine walk with You.

## 7-25
### Character Revelations
Our character sometimes has issues at deeper levels than we want to admit. Stress can bring out actions that are really manifestations of something in us that we did not know was in there. We may even be surprised at ourselves. We must face and take responsibility for these actions. When something surfaces from

deep within, it is an opportunity to cry out for a deeper cleansing of our inner self. In this way, our character is being constantly refined.

"Search me, O God, and know my heart; test me and know my thoughts. See if there is any wicked way in me, and lead me in the way everlasting." Psalm 139:23-24 (NRSV)


## 7-26
### The Universal Christ
We do not own Christ. He does not restrict His work to Christians only. Prevenient grace goes out to all mankind = the Holy Spirit works in all human hearts = the Universal Christ is drawing all persons to Himself. Jesus Christ is Lord of all (Acts 10:36). There is "One God and Father of all, who is above all and through all and in all" (Ephesians 4:6 NRSV). "In all"! Believing this changes how we see Christ. We must move beyond our tribal, local, provincial Christ to the Universal Christ who is in conquest of the whole world (Isaiah 11:9, Psalm 2, Zechariah 9:9-10). As we go, at home or abroad, know that He is already at work in every person you encounter.

"There is no longer Greek and Jew, circumcised and uncircumcised, barbarian, Scythian, slave and free; but Christ is all and in all!" Colossians 3:10-11 (NRSV)


## 7-27
### The Energy of Christ
Christ is energy, grace and love that flows into our lives from our Father. Life is difficult. The commands of Christ to love enemies and forgive those who have trespassed against us cannot be done in our own strength. God never expects us to do it on our own. When Christ is in us, the energy of God is working in us. It is by this energy that we obey, serve and live the cruciform. You do not have to do it on your own. You can't. In the energy of Christ you can.

"For I can do everything through Christ, who gives me strength (Philippians 4:13 NLT).

**7-28**
**Change Your Mind**
Ancient Israel was set on a land bridge that connected three continents on the Fertile Crescent. God set them there to be a light to the nations about the kingdom of God. However, their hunger to be like the other nations who had a king and the lure of that politic kept them from being the kingdom to which they were called. The lure of politics brought them down to the level of the other nations. They got their king with his kind of government. In time, Jesus Messiah came to reset the whole project with the words, "Change your minds (i.e. repent) the Kingdom of God is at hand." He still calls His kingdom people to avoid the pull of the world and be the light of the world (Matthew 5:14), showing the world what it looks like to live under the government of God.

"The LORD said to Samuel, 'Listen to the voice of the people in regard to all that they say to you, for they have not rejected you, but they have rejected Me from being king over them.'" 1 Samuel 8:7 (NASB)

**7-29**
**"Ain't-it-awful"**
"Ain't-it-awful" is one of the games people play. It is not a harmless game. Watch how often it happens when people are gathered together. Someone enters a rant about all the abounding sins of the surrounding culture, of a particular group, or some action of a person, present or past. Why do we make these speeches? Is it to make us feel better about ourselves or look better by way of contrast? Do we see our sins as worse than theirs or their sins worse than ours? We are all flawed. God loves all and is working by grace in all. Let that change your thinking and your speeches.

"For God did not send his Son into the world to condemn the world, but in order that the world might be saved through him." John 3:17 (ESV)

**7-30**
**Resisting Grace**
Resisting the Holy Spirit is way more than disobedience. At the heart of this sin is resisting His grace, and its unceasing flow through us. We were all meant to be channels of grace, showing to the world God's true character. How then do we resist? We do so by failing to give the same flow of grace to others that God

is flowing toward us. "Working together with Christ, then, we appeal to you not to receive the grace of God in vain" (2 Corinthians 6:1 ESV). Grace is "in vain" when it stops with us. We resist grace by holding those sinners, the ones that we classify as "the worst", at arm's length. We do so by taking our self-righteous seats and making our "ain't-it-awful" speeches. We are not here to curse the darkness, but to allow grace to flow from us to the darkness. Grace has Light in it. The world will continue to stumble in the dark until the flow of our harsh words are replaced with letting grace flow.

## 7-31
### Living By Dying
There is a way of living that ends in death. There is a way of dying that ends in life. There is a way of dying and living that looks like the dying and living of Christ. There is a kind of solidarity with Christ that brings life, health and wholeness. There is a place where the old self dies and the new self is born. There is a place where the faithfulness of Christ has become my faith and faithfulness toward Him. Oh, Spirit of Christ, keep bringing us to that place.

"I am crucified with Christ. I am, however, alive - but it isn't me any longer; it's the Messiah who lives in me. And the life I do still live in the flesh I live within the faithfulness of the son of God who loved me and gave himself for me." Galatians 2:20 (KNT)

## 8-1
### Examining Anger
Human nature can be strange. A person can be irritated or angry about one person or situation and transfer it to another person or situation; sometimes this is subconscious. We live in a time of lots of angry people; we see it everywhere. The Christian is to examine herself or himself and ask, "What am I really angry about?" "Why am I hurting my good name and my Christian witness by my anger?" "Do I let the sun go down on my anger and thus give the devil a foothold in my life (Ephesians 4:26-27)? Is the Spirit's fruit of self-control ruling my emotional life? Know that, "The anger of man does not achieve the righteousness of God" (James 1:20). It does little or nothing to advance Jesus' cause in the world.

Lord, restore the fruit of the Spirit in our lives. Enable us by grace and discipline to turn away from wrongful anger. May we know that our anger does little to advance your kingdom and rule among humankind. In the name of the Prince of Peace we pray. Amen.


## 8-2
### Jesus And Immigrants

Israel immigrated to Egypt; they received hospitality, food, and were given work; they thrived there for centuries before the arrival of an unknowing pharaoh (Exodus 1: 8). There are many stories of people migrations throughout ancient and Biblical history. They were either fleeing violence or food shortages in search of something better for themselves and especially their families. Jesus' family immigrated to Egypt to escape the violence of Herod and were refugees there. Jesus descended from a Moabite immigrant (Matthew 1:5); her name was Ruth. She received hospitality and food from Boaz and was protected by him from exploitation and likely rape as she worked in the fields (Ruth 2:9, 22). The hospitality that Israel received became a command of hospitality for all succeeding generations of God's kingdom citizens.

"When a stranger resides with you in your land, you shall not do him wrong. The stranger who resides with you shall be to you as the native among you, and you shall love him as yourself, for you were aliens in the land of Egypt; I am the LORD your God." Leviticus 19:33-34 (NASB)


## 8-3
### Blessed Assurance

Assurance must be more than a theological proposition of, "If I do A, and B, then C is sure". True Christian assurance is set forth in Scripture, not as a formula but as an inner witness. God has put His Spirit inside of the believer. The Spirit inside the believer addresses God as "Abba, Father!" It now knows itself as God's child and is inwardly assured as such. "For you have not received a spirit of slavery leading to fear again, but you have received a spirit of adoption as sons by which we cry out, "Abba! Father!" The Spirit Himself testifies with our spirit that we are children of God" (Romans 8:15-16 NASB).

## 8-4
### The Glowing Path
"Footprints of Jesus, that make the pathway glow; we will follow the steps of Jesus where'er they go" (Mrs. M. B. Slade). Jesus is, "The true light, which enlightens everyone, was coming into the world" (John 1:9 NRSV). Looking directly at a strong light will destroy your eyes. Light is given to enable us to see all other things. Jesus is the Light that makes us see right from wrong in a whole new way. He is the Light that dispels inadequate views of Father God. The light of the cross shows us how to deal with suffering, persecution and rejection. His pure light exposes our masks, our excuses and our unloving deeds. Let His light shine on your pathway and you will always know how to walk.


## 8-5
### Knowledge And Wisdom
"Many shall run to and fro, and knowledge shall increase" (Daniel 12:4b ESV). We live in a time of a great information explosion. It is so tremendous that it is intimidatingly overwhelming. Somehow we think that we are the wisest people who ever walked the earth. Not so! Knowledge and wisdom are not the same. Wisdom processes knowledge and arrives at truth along with proper courses of action. The wisdom of the world does not lead us to God, but the wisdom of Christ does.

"Where is the one who is wise? Where is the scribe? Where is the debater of this age? Has not God made foolish the wisdom of the world? For since, in the wisdom of God, the world did not know God through wisdom, it pleased God through the folly of what we preach to save those who believe." 1 Corinthians 1:20-21 (ESV)


## 8-6
### Making The Unknown Known
In Acts 17:22-31 is the story of Paul's sermon on Mar's Hill about the *Image to the Unknown God*. In this sermon Paul reminded pagans that they were children of God; that their very existence was tied to the hidden Christ whom they had not yet come to confess, though "He is not far from each one of us." Their very lives were sustained by the One whom they had not yet come to know. What if our evangelism was a reminder to embrace the One who is already at work in the lives of the ones to whom we witness? What if we helped them see that the One

at work in their hearts is the same incarnate One who went to the cross to redeem us all?

"That they would seek God, if perhaps they might grope for Him and find Him, though He is not far from each one of us; for in Him we live and move and exist, as even some of your own poets have said, 'For we also are His children'." Acts 17:27-28 (NASB)

## 8-7
### Grace And Truth
"For the law was given through Moses; grace and truth came through Jesus Christ" (John 1:17). The law announced condemnation; grace announces love and mercy. The law could not change us but love and grace could. The law revealed truth as a moral code; grace revealed Truth as a Person. The law was preparatory, awaiting the fullness of grace. The incarnation (life-of-God-in-flesh-among-us) demonstrated Jesus Messiah was one that was "full of grace and truth" (1:14). Grace is God's attitude toward us and His energy at work in us. To receive Him is to receive embodied Truth and grace piled on top of grace (1:16).

"And the Word became flesh and dwelt among us, and we have seen his glory, glory as of the only Son from the Father, full of grace and truth...For from his fullness we have all received, grace upon grace. For the law was given through Moses; grace and truth came through Jesus Christ. No one has ever seen God; the only God, who is at the Father's side, he has made him known." John 1:14, 16-18 (ESV)

## 8-8
### Follow The Pattern
Whenever you are building something it always helps if you have an example to go by. It also helps if you have a helper. When we are building our life as workers together with God, the Father has sent the Son so that we will have Someone by which we can pattern our lives. The Spirit in us will testify of Him and keep pointing our lives unceasingly to this likeness that is being uniquely recreated in us. Read His words, look long at Him in meditation, prayer and communion. This shaping process is that to which He called you.

"When the Helper comes, whom I will send to you from the Father, that is the Spirit of truth who proceeds from the Father, He will testify about Me" John 15:26.

## 8-9
### The Divine Likeness
The Son of God became fully human by incarnation. He became human to show us in flesh and blood what God is like and thus at the same time show us what we are to be like. God is like Jesus. Jesus was the ideal human. That is what Jesus came to show us. We are to be like Jesus and thus like God; the plan is to be restored in the Divine Likeness. He sends the Third member of the Holy Trinity, the Holy Spirit, who is Himself God, to live in us, to make us like God, and to prepare us to be joined to God.

"And we, who with unveiled faces all reflect the Lord's glory, are being transformed into his likeness with ever-increasing glory, which comes from the Lord, who is the Spirit." 2 Corinthians 3:18 (NIV)

## 8-10
### The Saving Serpent
We associate the serpent with the old tempting serpent in Eden. Moses used a serpent on a pole to save Israel from the bites of serpents in the wilderness. Who would ever think of a serpent being the symbol of Christ on the cross? Who would ever think that the One who did not sin became sin? Who would have thought that by looking at the uplifted serpent one could live? Indeed, He does free us from the bite of sin! Indeed, we can "Look and Live; look to Jesus now and live". The uplifted One delivers us from death! In Him we are healed!

"As Moses lifted up the serpent in the wilderness, even so must the Son of Man be lifted up; so that whoever believes will in Him have eternal life." John 3:14-15 (NASB)

## 8-11
### Loathsome Bread
In the wilderness the Exodus crowd came to despise the manna that was keeping them alive. To them it had become loathsome; it was not that on which they would have chosen to dine. In John 6 the thought of eating the flesh of the

Son of God was also loathsome, though Jesus reminded them that to eat the Bread of Heaven is to have eternal life. This Bread is given for the life of the world. Many disciples went away at that loathsome thought. Millions today rejoice at the Eucharistic table with these words, "Take eat, this is my body."

"After this many of his disciples turned back and no longer walked with him. So Jesus said to the Twelve, "Do you want to go away as well?" Simon Peter answered him, "Lord, to whom shall we go? You have the words of eternal life, and we have believed, and have come to know, that you are the Holy One of God." John 6:66-69 (ESV)

## 8-12
### Tell The Story
The story of Jesus is the greatest story ever told. Tell it, for so many have never heard. It is life changing. It is the story of incarnation, the story of the manger, the story of the cross and the story of resurrection. It is the story that has the power to change our lives and our own story. It is the story of a better way to live. Tell the story with your words, your actions and your reactions. Keep your life centered in Christ and His story and live out of that Center; that within itself will tell the story.

## 8-13
### The Sovereignty of God
To say that God directed Hitler to kill Jews, or devises that a toddler drowns in the swimming pool, or selects a dump truck to run over a laughing-playing child, or has designed at this point in history to have gun toters enter schools and mass murder children, or engineers human trafficking, along with a thousand other evils, all are absurd preposterous attacks on the holy character of God. (If God controls all things we cannot lift our voice against anything — absolutely nothing!) Know this, evil cannot spring out of the heart of a God whom Jesus has revealed as "God is Love". God does not play both sides of the chess board, making all human choices an illusion. No matter what happens on your chess board with whatever evil is seeking to destroy you, GOD'S SOVEREIGNTY MEANS THAT HE IS NEVER LEFT WITHOUT A MOVE TO MAKE ALL THINGS WORK TOGETHER FOR GOOD IN YOUR LIFE!! WHO ELSE CAN DO THAT? GOD ALONE!

Our Father, thank You for taking the things in our lives that we thought would be our very undoing to be our making. To You, Oh God, belong glory and majesty forever. Amen.

## 8-14
### Increasing Love
Love by nature grows and knows increase. Since the essence of holiness is love, then sanctification is that process of responding to light and grace where we love more and more. It is to discover new ways to love. It is to intentionally move ourselves in healthier ways to affirm and embrace all the objects of God's love. We know how broad and inclusive that is!

"And this is my prayer, that your love may overflow more and more with knowledge and full insight to help you to determine what is best, so that in the day of Christ you may be pure and blameless, having produced the harvest of righteousness that comes through Jesus Christ for the glory and praise of God." Philippians 1:9-11 (NRSV)

## 8-15
### Seven Ways To Emotional Anxiety
    Try to please everyone.
    Try to change other people.
    Try to fix other people.
    Try to compare yourself to others.
    Try to take responsibility for other people's actions.
    Try to change the past by your regrets.
    Try to carry tomorrow's burdens today.

"So do not worry about tomorrow; for tomorrow will care for itself. Each day has enough trouble of its own" Matthew 6:34 (NASB). "So Peter seeing him *said to Jesus, "Lord, and what about this man?" Jesus *said to him, "If I want him to remain until I come, what is that to you? You follow Me!"' John 21:21-22 (NASB)

## 8-16
### Disobeying The "Yes"
Disobedience is to say "Yes" to that to which God says "No". We understand that one, and have got it down pat. But we have forgotten that disobedience is to say

"No" to that to which God says "Yes". God has a "Yes" to compassion, doing justice, practicing kindness, giving grace, showing mercy, helping the weak, and caring for the last and least of these. The Bible affirms these in both OT and NT. Having reduced Christianity to moralism, we have neglected doing high priority things for lesser things (Matthew 23:23, Luke 11:42). If it is a "Yes" project for our Father, then it must be at the top of our to-do list.

## 8-17
### Unable To Hear
When I look back on my life I am saddened by what I should have heard, and could have heard, if my ways of thinking had not been so entrenched. When new truth comes to us it is important to be open, pause and listen to this new truth, or else all we will hear is our old ways of seeing, distorting what is needing and begging to be heard. We hear what we want to hear and see what we want to see. That is scary when it comes to the truth that comes from our speaking Lord.

"Anyone with ears to hear should listen and understand." Then he added, "Pay close attention to what you hear. The closer you listen, the more understanding you will be given—and you will receive even more." Mark 4:23-24 (NLT)

## 8-18
### It Comes Back
"Judge not, and you will not be judged; condemn not, and you will not be condemned; forgive, and you will be forgiven; give, and it will be given to you. Good measure, pressed down, shaken together, running over, will be put into your lap. For with the measure you use it will be measured back to you." Luke 6:37-38 (ESV). It's the law of sowing and reaping! You get treated like you treat others! It comes back to you. Giving generous grace is the best way to live.

## 8-19
### Choices And Character
We do not always get to decide what to do based on a voice from God. Yet God expects us to make good decisions. It seems that God is into shaping character toward maturity. Character shapes decisions and decisions build character. In this regard, He then does not tell us everything to do. He gave us the examples

of OT and NT and foremost that of Christ Himself, the flowing love of the Spirit, and the overflowing grace of the Father as means of grace to make life's decisions. It all calls for the use of our mind, examining the intent of our heart and checking out our motives. Character is shaped by that process.

## 8-20
### It's Forgiven
Regretting some past sin that has already been forgiven? You cannot change it You do not need to bear that! Christ already has! "He himself bore our sins in his body on the tree, so that we might die to sins and live for righteousness" (1 Peter 2:24a NIV). You are forgiven. Don't go back there! Surely, don't dwell there. Instead, the Book is reminding us to die to all sin. By grace, crucify them all. They are past, so keep them that way. Bury what is dead and move on.

## 8-21
### A Mind Changing Transformation
"Change your mind, the Kingdom of Heaven is here." This was the first message of John the Baptist, Jesus and His disciples. It was the Gospel, and still is; the good news is that the rule of King Jesus has arrived and He is Lord of the whole earth. "But we thought Rome had to be gone first". Change your mind! 'Isn't our first loyalty to our national government?" Change your mind! "Isn't that a little subversive?" Yes! It got John the Baptist and Paul beheaded, and Jesus crucified. "Can't the Kingdom be the same as the national government?" Change your mind! Constantine already tried that. "Isn't it just a spiritual kingdom that we hold in our hearts?" Change your mind! It will affect most everything we do and think. It calls for us to reorder our priorities. "Seek first God's rule and reign among you, along with His righteousness (i.e. Jesus' teachings, compassionate mercy, restorative justice.) and all you need will be added to you" (Paraphrase of Matthew 6:33). Change your mind! It's time to live, "Thy kingdom come, thy will be done, on earth as it is in Heaven."

## 8-22
### Please Discern
Often when the Bible speaks of not judging it has to do with not condemning. There is, however, a judging that is necessary. It is a kind of evaluating between good and evil, right and wrong, and better and best. There is a kind of judging

that the church must do in church discipline. There is a kind of judging that seeks to know the difference between true prophets and false prophets by their good fruit and bad fruit (Matthew 7:15-20). We judge (discern) between spirits: "Every spirit is not from God" I John 4:1-6. Use your mind. Listen to the Spirit. It will help us get through lots of mine fields.

"Woe to those who call evil good and good evil, who put darkness for light and light for darkness, who put bitter for sweet and sweet for bitter." Isaiah 5:20 (NIV)

## 8-23
### Science And The Bible
Some Christians are only interested in theology and "Bible doctrine". There should not be fear from Christians about other sciences. Psychology, biology, physics, and other sciences need not contradict good theology. Truth cannot contradict truth. Sometimes, interpreting everything in the Bible as literal unnecessarily drives bright minds away from the Bible and the church. What is true in the sciences need not drive us away from the Bible. The study of this planet, the universe and its galaxies, the human body and psyche, animals and plants are all studies in what God has made. All truth is derived from God and all truth is God's truth. None of us possess truth fully or completely. We are disciples following Jesus and the world He created and sustains (Colossians 1:15-17). Do not try to put Him in your little restrictive box and foolishly think you contain Him or can explain Him. He who has been around billions time billions of light years before we were born cannot be crammed into our little calendars. We have made our God and His Christ way too small. Forgive us, Holy One!

"Who is this that darkens counsel by words without knowledge? Gird up your loins like a man, I will question you, and you shall declare to me. Where were you when I laid the foundation of the earth? Tell me, if you have understanding." Job 38:2-4 (NRSV) (See Job 38-39).

## 8-24
### No Chummy God
Jesus taught us to address God as Father in our prayers. Father speaks of close familial relationship. But Jesus also taught us to say, "Our Father, hallowed be thy name." Our Father is beyond chummy; He is holy. We are to come to Him with complete reverence and high awe. We are never to bring Him down to the

level of a mere buddy. The one who is our Friend is also exalted, high and lifted up. Yet, He is our Father who desires to be near to His children.

"God, the blessed and only Ruler, the King of kings and Lord of lords, who alone is immortal and who lives in unapproachable light, whom no one has seen or can see. To him be honor and might forever. Amen." 1 Timothy 6:15b-16 (NIV)

## 8-25
### My Forgiveness and Forgiving
Compare the Lord's prayer in Matthew 6:12 and Luke.11:4: "Forgive us our debts, <u>as we also have forgiven</u> our debtors" (Matthew 6:12 (ESV). This is even stronger in (Luke 11:4 ESV) "Forgive us our sins, <u>for we ourselves forgive everyone</u> who is indebted to us." We need to forgive to be forgiven. The forgiven must forgive. We ask the Father for forgiveness as we have and while we are forgiving each other. In Matthew, Jesus reinforces the whole prayer by adding, "For if you forgive others their trespasses, your heavenly Father will also forgive you, but if you do not forgive others their trespasses, neither will your Father forgive your trespasses" (Matthew 6:14-15 ESV). In the same way we cannot claim we love God while not loving our brother, neither can we claim a forgiveness from God to us that does not flow out to others. That's sobering! If sanctification is being restored to the divine likeness, we cannot be like God without forgiving. Being a forgiving person is one of the best ways we can represent God in the world.

## 8-26
### Discover The Hunger
We must listen to our own souls. Inside of us is a deep hunger for prayer intimacy with God. It longs to be alone in conversation with Him. It longs to pray with others. Nothing will satisfy this hunger like times alone talking with Him. Stop ignoring the hunger. Stop shoving junk food toward it. The soul is hungry for its Father. It longs for Him like a baby longs for its mother's breast. It longs for Him like lovers long for each other. Only God can fill this life-long hunger. Fixes will not fix it. He can. He wants to. He is waiting for your longing to meet His longing. This is where hunger is satisfied. Listen to your own soul. Discover this hunger.

"As the deer pants for the water brooks, So my soul pants for You, O God. My soul thirsts for God, for the living God" Psalm 42:1-2a (NASB).

## 8-27
### Trust the Spirit
The Spirit leads. He speaks. He calls. He guides. Let Him speak to you. Listen to Him. Sometimes He speaks through a deep gut feeling. Since we are co-laborers with Him, and He is inside us, we may question, "Is that me or is that the Spirit"? Listen. Pray. Act. Trust the Spirit. Sometimes He puts you in the middle of a situation to be His ministering agent. Sometimes we have only a few moments to act with Him in ministering love. Don't miss His timing. Learn to live in this realm not merely occasionally but perpetually. No, it won't be a miracle a minute, but it will be a life that will touch others for God.

"For all who are being led by the Spirit of God, these are sons of God" Romans 8:14 (NASB)

## 8-28
### Pray With The Spirit
We are called to pray with Spirit as the Spirit prays through us. Pray until you hear the Spirit praying through you. This is hearing from Heaven. Pray until your asking is changed to what He wants; "we do not know how to pray as we ought". "If you abide in me, and my words abide in you, ask whatever you wish, and it will be done for you." (John 15:7 ESV). The Spirit in us is the abiding Word. He reinforces the words of Christ. When these words shape our desires and wishes, our praying goes to a whole new level. This is praying with the Spirit.

"Likewise the Spirit helps us in our weakness; for we do not know how to pray as we ought, but that very Spirit intercedes with sighs too deep for words. And God, who searches the heart, knows what is the mind of the Spirit, because the Spirit intercedes for the saints according to the will of God" Romans 8:26-27 (NRSV).

## 8-29
### Receiving Confession
"Therefore, confess your sins to one another, and pray for one another so that you may be healed" James 5:16a. Have you ever received a confession of sin?

Did you hear with grace and compassion? Did you keep it confidential? Did you affirm forgiveness? The above verse is little practiced but greatly needed. Believers need someone to whom they can bare their souls. We need spiritual mentors who will hear, understand and give us grace and encouragement to go on. We are a kingdom of priests, you know.

"But you are a chosen people, a royal priesthood, a holy nation, a people belonging to God, that you may declare the praises of him who called you out of darkness into his wonderful light." 1 Peter 2:9 (NIV)

## 8-30
### All Kinds of Greed
In the NT greed was taken seriously. Paul forbade the church to associate with or fellowship with a greedy person (1 Corinthians 5:11). The church throughout its history has patronized greedy persons because of its own greed. Jesus said, "Watch out! Be on your guard against all kinds of greed" (Luke 12:15). "Love of money is at the root of all kinds of evil" (1 Timothy 6:10). Greed takes many forms. Theft. Covetousness. Gambling. Lawsuits. Injustice. Manipulation. Oppression. More. Bigger. Better, and a thousand other things. God's people are to guard their hearts and actions against all kinds of greed. It is very difficult to do in a consumer society with all of its abundance. Work it out, with "fear and trembling."

## 8-31
### Pilate's Politics
The words, "If you let this Man go, you are not Caesar's friend" (John 19:12) struck terror in the soul of Pilate. Three times he had said, "I find no fault in him." (John 18:38, 19:4, 19:6) but now his politics "forced" him to crucify the promised Messiah, King of the world. His political future rested on being Caesar's friend. He washed his hands showing he believed Jesus was an innocent man (Matthew 27:24). He did nothing to stop the crucifixion; his hand washing was the green light to let the crucifixion proceed. Jesus suffered under Pilate's politics. His teachings are still nailed to the tree because we so much want to be a friend of Caesar. His kingdom teachings are far too radical for the kingdoms of this world so we act like "we have no king but Caesar".

"From then on Pilate sought to release Him, but the Jews cried out, saying, "If you let this Man go, you are not Caesar's friend. Whoever makes himself a king speaks against Caesar.".... "Pilate said to them, "Shall I crucify your King?" The chief priests answered, 'We have no king but Caesar!'" John 19:12, 15 (NKJV).

### 9-1
**Prayer Is An Act of Love**
In prayer we love on our Father and He loves on us; prayer is intimacy with God. Prayer is where we work on the relationship; it is where we receive forgiveness for the things that have hindered the relationship. In prayer we love on folks by our intercession for them. Praying for enemies is an act of love that transforms the pray-er to be more loving. Prayer is the secret place that prepares our own hearts to love as we go from the prayer closet into the arena of life with all of its interactions.

"Let all who seek You rejoice and be glad in You; Let those who love Your salvation say continually, 'The LORD be magnified!'" Psalm 40:16 (NASB)

### 9-2
**Discover Praying Out Loud**
In your own prayer life, learn to pray aloud. Spoken words in prayer commit us in ways that thinking our prayers do not. These can be whispered prayers; whispers are spoken words, too. Spoken prayers can have a humble boldness in them. It changes "just thinking" into praying. It helps hold wandering thoughts in check. It gives verbal expression to our petition and becomes a statement of faith. Spoken words have the power of faith or the power of doubt in them. Our faith is not in our own words but in the Lord to whom the words are spoken.

"As for me, I will call upon God, And the LORD shall save me. Evening and morning and at noon I will pray, and cry aloud, And He shall hear my voice." Psalm 55:16-17 (NKJV)

### 9-3
**On Being Intentional**
It has been said, "The road to hell is paved with good intentions." That is only so because the good intentions were never acted upon. Our intentions to do all

manner of good can come to be if we have a plan to act on the intentions. Procrastination is not the friend of action. Solution? It involves setting the time to pray, to study, to visit the sick, care for human need and a thousand other good things. It involves writing it down, putting it on the calendar and getting on with it. Intentional living. Intentional discipleship.

Father, may we not allow our good intentions to lull us away from doing actual deeds of righteousness. Amen!

## 9-4
### Intercession
Both Christ and the Spirit intercede for us (Romans 8:26, 34). Yet we are urged to offer "supplications, prayers, intercessions, and thanksgivings for all people" (1 Timothy 2:1). This is more than participation in intercession. Is there an intercession where the Spirit is interceding through the intercessors? If so, would this not be the highest form of intercession? The true intercessor does not march into the prayer closet with his or her lists for asking. We are to be so open to what the Spirit is praying that it changes our praying; when this happens, we are now praying what the Intercessor is praying.

## 9-5
### Race Supremacy
No race is superior to another race. We are all made in the divine likeness. We are all humans designed by a loving Creator to love each other. True, there are skin and cultural differences, but the God who bridged all gaps to come to us in Christ has modeled what we must do and be for all human beings. Instead of deeming ourselves better, we are to deem all others as better than ourselves (Philippians 2:3-4). We are not to lord it over anyone, but we are to make ourselves the servants of all. Find ways to love and serve and see what happens to your heart. If we sit where others sit until we feel what they feel, then we will wonder at our past thoughtlessness.

## 9-6
### Divisions And Unity
There are divisions that are caused by Christ (Luke 12:49-56) and there are divisions that are healed by Christ. Following Christ may bring divisions with

friends and family. But there are divisions that are to be bridged between fellow Christians and other fellow humans by love for the sake of Christ. Even those who have rejected us because of our faith are to still be the objects of our love and the subjects of our prayers. God desires ultimate unity of the whole human family around His Son, who came to reconcile the world to God. We follow Him by peace-making, unity and reconciliation.

"God was in Christ reconciling the world to Himself, not counting their trespasses against them, and He has committed to us the word of reconciliation." 2 Corinthians 5:19 (NASB)

## 9-7
### Feeling Stones
A childhood friend said to me one time, "Do you remember throwing rocks at us?" My reply was "No". He said, "Well, I remember it!" I have never forgotten the lessons of that short conversation. We do remember stones thrown our way. If you were ever rejected, discriminated against, hated, abused sexually, abused physically, put down, cast aside, ridiculed or hurt by one of a thousand stones, you know it and remember it. There are those in our world with whom we must identify and feel their pain if they would ever hear about our Christ. Our patient love can prepare the way for others to hear of His love. Folks can't believe our statement, "God loves you" if we don't love them.

## 9-8
### Love Inspires Good
God does not force people to obey his own laws. Though His laws are against it, He does not stop those who are determined to use God's name in vain, worship idols, steal, kill, destroy, commit adultery, bear false witness, and covet. He pursues us in love, but does not force. Paul reminds us that the law cannot change a person. Our forcing is futile; it misrepresents God, along with the Christ of the gospel. God's energy, called love and grace, wants to draw all persons to Himself; "He is not willing that any should perish". Since God does not force people, neither should we. His overtures of love draw and inspire, so should ours.

## 9-9
### Contempt
Nothing is more devastating to the human psyche than contempt. It has a far worse impact than hate or anger. It creates deep divisions and lifelong enemies. Contempt expresses itself in putting people down, demonizing them and calling them names because they do not agree with your ideas. Contempt is now rampant. It is the reason we cannot have civil discourse about differing ideas on any subject. Once an idea or opinion is put forth the person or group are railed against in devastating and contemptuous ways. The only cure is to love your enemies. Love those whose ideas you don't embrace. Listen in love to differing opinions. We do not have to be right, but we must love.

"You're familiar with the command to the ancients, 'Do not murder.' I'm telling you that anyone who is so much as angry with a brother or sister is guilty of murder. Carelessly call a brother 'idiot!' and you just might find yourself hauled into court. Thoughtlessly yell 'stupid!' at a sister and you are on the brink of hellfire. The simple moral fact is that words kill." Matthew 5:21-22 (MSG)

## 9-10
### Be Good, Do Good
If you want to be good then go out into the world and do good. Do good, not to be seen by the camera, but to be seen by your Father (Matthew 6:4). This world is in need of sheer goodness, salt-of-the-earth goodness, light of the world goodness. Jesus commissioned his followers to do good works. "Let your light shine before men in such a way that they may see your good works, and glorify your Father who is in heaven" (Matthew 5:16 NASB).

Barnabas "was a good man, full of the Holy Spirit and faith, and a great number of people were brought to the Lord." Acts 11:24 (NIV)

## 9-11
### Gather Eternal Fruit
We can all gather eternal fruit. We do it by planting eternal seeds in the hearts and minds of folks in our sphere of influence. We do it by acts of kindness and works of mercy. We do it by showing grace and having true concern. It is prayer and care. It is visiting and listening. It is a verbal witness and a silent deed. Someday we will see the fruit in the persons we touched, who are in the Eternal

City because of our influence. And we will give God glory that we were laborers together in His vineyard.

"The one who plants and the one who waters have a common purpose, and each will receive wages according to the labor of each. For we are God's servants, working together; you are God's field, God's building." 1 Corinthians 3:8-9 (NRSV)

## 9-12
### The Rebuilt Temple
The old temple, where God and humans met, was destroyed in 70 AD. Jesus had the new temple already in place 37 years before Herod's temple was destroyed. Jesus is the temple. "Destroy this temple, and in three days I will raise it up" (John 2:19). The NT church saw Jesus as being the new place where God and man met (i.e. the new tent of meeting, (Exodus 40:34-35); Jesus is now where the temple shekinah glory dwells (John 1:14). We have no other temple; we look for no other. The only temple we have now is Jesus; the only temple in our future is Jesus. "I saw no temple in the city, for its temple is the Lord God the Almighty and the Lamb" (Revelation 21:22 NRSV). Hallelujah to the Lamb!

A paraphrase of John 1:14. "And God became human coming as our temple (tabernacle) among us, and the glory that rested on the temple rested on Him, He was the only begotten from the Father; He was full of grace and truth." Commentary: He now has become our temple, fully God and fully man, the Father's Way to us and our Way to the Father. In Him heaven and earth, God and human have perfectly met. Wow! What a Temple!

## 9-13
### Refillings Of The Spirit
The refilling of the Spirit is for one reason. It is not so you can chalk up another spiritual experience or a new emotional high. Never! The Father is not the least bit interested in giving you the Spirit for narcissistic reasons. He wants to give the Spirit so that you may again witness with boldness, so that you as a temple, a dwelling place of the Spirit (I Corinthians 3:16) can return to the world in the power of the Spirit to touch other humans with the life of God which dwells in you.

"And when they had prayed, the place where they had gathered together was shaken, and they were all filled with the Holy Spirit and began to speak the word of God with boldness." Acts 4:31 (NASB)

## 9-14
### Love's Demands

Love requires a response. Love places a burden on us. It does not force us, or it would not be love. Love moves us. We want to do something in response; that is love's demand. It calls receivers to be givers. It calls the disinterested to be interested. It calls bystanders to be participants. It demands my whole life to be given back to God in service and worship. Such amazing love calls for my all and my best.

"For the love of Christ urges us on, because we are convinced that one has died for all; therefore all have died. And he died for all, so that those who live might live no longer for themselves, but for him who died and was raised for them." 2 Corinthians 5:14-15 (NRSV)

## 9-15
### Subtle Sectarianism

There is a blatant sectarianism that is repulsive in all of its superior tribal claims. But never forget that there is a subtle sectarianism that has clothed itself in a deceptive sheep's coat. It is the feeling that my tribe is better than yours. It is the innuendo that suggests the other ones are less sincere than are we, less biblical than us and less committed. It is an attitude, a sorry disposition, a discriminating thought, a divisive slight; all attempts to hide itself from others and ourselves by denial. It is a sectarianism that is shrewd, but sectarian nonetheless. Its cure? Give the benefit of the doubt. Know that they are God's children too. Know the Father loves them in the same way He does you. Know that they may be just as sincere and committed as we are, maybe more.

"John answered, 'Master, we saw someone casting out demons in your name, and we tried to stop him, because he does not follow with us.' But Jesus said to him, 'Do not stop him; for whoever is not against you is for you.'" Luke 9:49-50 (NRSV)

## 9-16
### Disobedience And Satan
There is a spirit that encourages disobedience and is involved in acts of disobedience. The one who tempted Jesus in the wilderness entices us to sin. These acts of disobedience are an opportunity for Satan to work further havoc in our lives. Disobedience is more than a choice. It corrupts us spiritually in ways we do not discern. It has spiritual consequences. Something evil is at work when we live in resistance to God's way.

"In which you used to live when you followed the ways of this world and of the ruler of the kingdom of the air, the spirit who is now at work in those who are disobedient." Ephesians 2:2 (NIV)

## 9-17
### Mystery Of The Gospel
Paul said, "Pray also for me, that whenever I open my mouth, words may be given me so that I will fearlessly make known the mystery of the gospel" (Ephesians 6:19 NIV). It was a two-fold request that "words may be given me" and "fearlessly make known the mystery of the gospel." The forces of the world were set to produce fear and intimidation in anyone who would dare proclaim the messiahship of Jesus and another kingdom. This mystery of the Gospel needs the prayers of the people and the inspiration of the Spirit to advance with persuasive power. The long-hidden mystery is now revealed. The day of the Kingdom has arrived.

## 9-18
### Undying Love
"Grace to all who love our Lord Jesus Christ with an undying love" (Ephesians 6:24 NIV). Our love for our Lord was born out of His love for us. The spark of His love has ignited a flame in our hearts that should never go out. His doggedly-persistent love toward us should stir us to faithful love toward Him. The One who rose from the dead, the ever living One, has caused us to be born from above. Now welling up in our souls is this unquenchable, unquieted, undiminished and undying love.

## 9-19
### Live And Walk In The Spirit
"If we live by the Spirit, let us also walk by the Spirit" (Galatians 5:25 NASB). The Spirit is our source of life and the basis of our walk with the Lord. Think of it: live and walk. Without living in the Spirit, we cannot walk right. Without His life being the driving force of our lives, we falter by the way. When you see someone who is truly walking in the Spirit, know that in the inner sanctum of their souls they are living in the Spirit. Catch the wind of the Spirit in your sail and let it carry you along.

## 9-20
### Leave It There
There are some things that we have to bear with the help of the Lord, and there are other things we have to learn how to leave with Him. The latter is not as easy as saying or writing it. Some problems and issues walk with us as awkward companions. Though they walk with us, they no longer distract us from the true Companion of our soul. We have to learn to leave with Him those things that never are truly gone from our lives.

## 9-21
### Transparency And Problems
Everything is not always rosy in our lives, and we should not lead others and even our own children to think otherwise. Problems are as common to others as they are to us. We may do a disservice to those who come behind us if they are never allowed to glance at our pain. This sharing can be in the form of personal conversation, prayer requests, testimony, or our Christian witness as to how our Lord has helped us. This calls for wisdom in what, how and when we share. Transparency can help another person who is also struggling at some point. Knowing that you don't have a problem-free existence can help a fellow human deal with their problems.

"Bear one another's burdens, and thereby fulfill the law of Christ." Galatians 6:2 (NASB)

## 9-22
### Holy, Holy, Holy
Worship does not begin when the congregants enter the sanctuary. Worship is going on in Heaven at all times. Isaiah looked into the heavenly realm, saw and heard it. "Holy, Holy, Holy, is the LORD of hosts, The whole earth is full of His glory" Isaiah 6:3 (NASB). John also saw and heard it (Revelation 4:8). Holy, Holy, Holy is the true tuning fork of worship. We must attune our worship to it. It will banish trivial and shallow worship. It will produce a holy awe that can make us tremble. It struck conviction and repentance in the heart of Isaiah. A true vision of our holy God will do the same for us.

## 9-23
### He Became Poor
The Eternal Son was rich, but He became poor. He chose poverty. Who would do that?! "For you know the generous act of our Lord Jesus Christ, that though he was rich, yet for your sakes he became poor, so that by his poverty you might become rich" (2 Corinthians 8:9 NRSV). Do we want to talk about Christlikeness now? When you do, never forget this component of it. All the riches of grace we enjoy is because of His poverty. Throughout Christian history, many Christians have chosen depravation so that in the long run they could enrich the lives of those who follow. There is also a poverty of spirit or deep humility that can enrich the lives of fellow Christians.

## 9-24
### A Saving Relationship
Salvation is far more than a gift. It is a saving relationship that we have entered. We enter it by faith and live it out by faith as a life of trust and obedience. Biblically, belief and faith are never mere past events in our lives that initiate a conversion. Belief and faith are present-active adherence to our Lord day by day and moment by moment. Yesterday's belief is a pitiful and false substitute for a present intimate relationship with our Lord. This is the relationship that saves and makes us thrive.

"Now I would remind you, brothers and sisters, of the good news that I proclaimed to you, which you in turn received, in which also you stand, through which also you are being saved, if you hold firmly to the message that I proclaimed to you—unless you have come to believe in vain." 1 Corinthians 15:1-2 (NRSV)

## 9-25
### Gideon As King
Gideon was a rare soul. He had an offer to be king before Saul and David. He was not hungry for power. "Only the Lord himself will rule over you." He knew who he was in the grand scheme of things. When we have truly bowed to the Lord our King, then we know that it would be blasphemy for us to have that place; further, we know no other person on the planet deserves the veneration of that place. To enthrone the Lord totally as our King cleanses the soul of having another king, while also orienting our lives to bless the rest of humanity.

"Then the Israelites said to Gideon, 'Rule over us, you and your son and your grandson also; for you have delivered us out of the hand of Midian.' Gideon said to them, 'I will not rule over you, and my son will not rule over you; the LORD will rule over you.'" Judges 8:22-23 (NRSV).

## 9-26
### Rejecting The King
God was reestablishing His Kingship through His only begotten Son. The Kingdom was mocked by those in political and religious authority. The robe was meant to jeer him. Thorns were meant to imitate a kingly crown. The cross was a cruel throne for one who would dare interject Himself into the established political order as King. The title over His cross was not meant for acclamation but for defamation. While God is seeking to establish His kingdom, we are busy working and trying to establish ours, or someone else's kingdom. That too is a form of rejecting our rightful King.

"My kingdom isn't the sort that grows in this world," replied Jesus. "If my kingdom were from this world, my supporters would have fought to stop me being handed over to the Judaeans. So, then, my kingdom is not the sort that comes from here. "So!" said Pilate. "You are a king, are you?... "I was born for this; I've come into the world for this" (John 18:36-37 "Kingdom New Testament").

9-27
**Dividing The Church**
In our day of polarization, careless words are said about church leaders that can be very hurtful to the person and divisive to the body of Christ. This often happens when someone behaves as a sniper, firing away at a pastor, either directly or by innuendo. We live in a hyper-critical environment. It is no small thing to attack the leaders of the church merely because they do not say everything the way you want them to say it. It is evil to divide the body. It is horrible to sow discord in the community of faith in the name of being right. God detests those who sow discord among brothers (Proverbs 6:9). Watch your own soul and words in this regard. Talk directly to your leaders and always pray earnestly for them. Respect the unity of the Spirit in the church. It is devotion to your Lord.

"I therefore, a prisoner for the Lord, urge you to walk in a manner worthy of the calling to which you have been called, with all humility and gentleness, with patience, bearing with one another in love, eager to maintain the unity of the Spirit in the bond of peace." Ephesians 4:1-3 (ESV)


9-28
**Somebody Done Somebody Wrong**
There is a line in a country music song which says, "Hey, won't you play another somebody-done-somebody-wrong songs." My answer to that is, "Don't"! We have all been done wrong at one time or another and it does not help us to keep wallowing in it. It brings all of those old feelings back to us. It does not heal; It does not help us let it go. It does not help us forgive. It makes victims out of us. It douses us with self-pity. Move on from those wrongs done to you, and give them no more power over you by singing about it.

"One thing I do: forgetting what lies behind and reaching forward to what lies ahead, I press on toward the goal for the prize of the upward call of God in Christ Jesus" (Philippians 3:13b-14).


9-29
**The Fruits Of Not Forgiving**
When we fail to forgive another, there are consequential fruits that come from it. (1) We fail to be seen as fully Christian in our witness. (2) It embitters our own

soul. (3) It spills over into our family, and our children become negatively influenced. They may even walk away from the Lord and the church because they too have not forgiven what "they did to us." Is nursing your hurt worth losing your kids? (4) It fractures and cripples the church. Whole congregations can get stuck in choosing sides, which poisons the life of community. (5) We forget that we have trespassed as well. (6) We do not practice the Lord's prayer to forgive us as we forgive others.

## 9-30
### Do Not Be Cheated
Do not let the world cheat you out of your death in Christ. The world will offer you false life and false reality so that you can run away from the death to which your Lord calls you. Take up your cross. Look carefully at your life in this world and you will find an opportunity to embrace this death. Out of this death, you will live. There is no life without it. Eternal life is the end result of this death to which you are being called (Philippians 3:10-11). "If we have died with him, we will also live with him" (2 Timothy 2:11b). We cheat ourselves if we miss it.

## 10-1
### Give Them Grace
Give others grace, and see what God does. Let the kindness of Christ flow through you. Let the peace that God has given your own soul bless someone else. Let the overflow of God's love in you spill out to create hunger in the hearts of those eating the pods of the pig pen. Do not meet anger with anger. Do not retort with harsher words than came at you. The enemy would love that. The Christ of grace has commissioned you as an ambassador of grace. May they feel a benediction of grace radiating from your life.

"The grace of the Lord Jesus Christ, and the love of God, and the communion of the Holy Spirit be with you all. Amen." 2 Corinthians 13:14 (NKJV)

## 10-2
### The Barking Dog
When I was a little boy, a barking dog rushed at me from beneath his owner's parked car and scared me so badly that I thought I was bitten. I had experienced no physical harm, but nevertheless tried to find a scar to prove the attack. The

enemy of our soul is a master at creating fear and intimidation. Do not give him the victory by believing his blusterous bark. Do not let his growls and howls defeat you. You belong to Jesus. Our Lord has already defeated the enemy. In Him, you overcome the evil one.

"For dogs have surrounded me; A band of evildoers has encompassed me; They pierced my hands and my feet." Psalm 22:16 (NASB)

## 10-3
### Live Closer
The closer we get to Jesus, the clearer is our vision of sin. His Light reveals where we are. The more we become like Christ, the more we realize how wide the gap is. The closer we get to Him, the wider the distance between us and Him seems. There is something about the nearness to holiness that makes us cry out as Isaiah did, "Woe is me." There is fullness of joy in being near Him; there is growth toward His likeness as we commune with Him. His Presence cleanses. His nearness revives. Though you will feel the distance, you will actually be living closer.

## 10-4
### The Spirit And Holiness
The Spirit calls us to holiness. He enables us in its pursuit. He Himself is the Reward of our entry into it. The call is God's invitation to be "partakers of the divine nature." The Spirit lifts up Jesus; the Spirit guides us in the Way of Holiness which is none other than Christ Himself. Holiness is not something in addition to Jesus, it is just more of Jesus. It is a passion to have more of Him while giving Him all of us. The Spirit has to be in the middle of that.

"For God did not call us to impurity but in holiness. Therefore whoever rejects this rejects not human authority but God, who also gives his Holy Spirit to you." 1 Thessalonians 4:7-8 (NRSV)

## 10-5
### Amazing Grace And The Spirit
Grace involves all members of the Holy Trinity. We often speak of the Father's grace and that of the Son, but we also must remember that the Holy Spirit is the

Spirit of amazing grace. He expresses the grace of the Father and the Son to us, but He also enables grace to flow out of us. We are sanctified by the Spirit of Grace (Hebrews 10:29). The evidence that we have received grace is an outflow of grace from our lives. We who have received grace as unearned mercy give unearned mercy. If the Spirit of Grace dwells in us, our lives will be full of the grace of our Lord.

Father, may we know that You have given us the Spirit to touch the world with Your grace. Amen.

## 10-6
### Getting Distracted
Distractions will make you miss your turn and get you on the wrong road. They can get you into unnecessary collisions. They show a loss of focus. They can make you miss opportunities. They move you away from the pursuit of your goals. To get back on the right way, distractions must be ignored, or put in their place. It means that you must become purposeful and focused. Our primary purpose as believers is to follow our Lord and to become like Him. So, to get back on the way we must turn our eyes again on Jesus.

## 10-7
### Identifying Mark
God is love. This is revealed by His actions. This is what the disciples learned about the Father from Jesus. This is who He is. It that yet us? It is what we are to become. We are to bear that DNA of the love of our Father, if we indeed derive our life from Him. "Beloved, let us love one another, for love is from God; and everyone who loves is born of God and knows God. The one who does not love does not know God, for God is love" (1 John 4:7-13 NASB). The Father's children are known by their love. The Disciples of Jesus are known by their love (John 13:35). It is what a Christian is. We have defined Christians too often by other identifying marks. When we are truly born from above, we will begin to embody love.

## 10-8
### The Gospel Of The Kingdom
We have washed the NT clean of the political implications of the Kingdom of God. We have done such a good job that what the first century hearers heard in

"Repent for God's Kingdom has arrived", we no longer hear, nor even understand. We have made bearing the cross something spiritually sterile. Early Christians bore their cross in non-violent opposition to the empire to their gory deaths. We are busy aligning ourselves with the kingdoms of men rather than establishing the rule of our King. We have changed the good news (gospel) into how to get a ticket to heaven. In the NT the meaning of the good news (gospel) is that God's rule has arrived (Mark 1:14-15).

"Later on, after John was arrested, Jesus went into Galilee, where he preached God's Good News. 'The time promised by God has come at last!' he announced. 'The Kingdom of God is near! Repent of your sins and believe the Good News!" Mark 1:14-15 (NLT)

## 10-9
### Disintegration Or Restoration
Our disordered passions end in disintegration. Unless we turn by repentance, that will end in death. "While we were living in the flesh, our sinful passions, aroused by the law, were at work in our members to bear fruit for death" (Romans 7:5 NRSV). The Father has given us the Son and the Spirit to lead us away from this path of death to the fullness of life. We owe Him everything because of this initiative. "So then, brothers and sisters, we are debtors, not to the flesh, to live according to the flesh—for if you live according to the flesh, you will die; but if by the Spirit you put to death the deeds of the body, you will live. For all who are led by the Spirit of God are children of God" (Romans 8:12-14 NRSV).

## 10-10
### Worst Moment
God knew us at our worst moment and still loved us. "God demonstrates His own love toward us, in that while we were yet sinners, Christ died for us" (Romans 5:8 NASB). He knows us better than we know ourselves and still reaches out to us with unconditional self-sacrificial love. Somehow, we think God sits totally absorbed with our past transgressions and all of our worst moments. He does not. He is more concerned with what we are becoming than with what we have been.

## 10-11
### Turn The Page
The teacher was reading a story to a young child. As soon as the child would hear the opened page read, she would say, "Turn the page, teacher. Turn the page." As we grow older, it may not always be easy to turn the page, but we must. The sad chapters of yesterday must not be allowed to spoil today's reading. When you start to get stuck over some old regret, tell yourself, "Turn the page. Turn the page."

"Whom God displayed publicly as a propitiation in His blood through faith. This was to demonstrate His righteousness, because in the forbearance of God He passed over the sins previously committed." Romans 3:25 (NASB)

## 10-12
### Our Sovereign Lord
God is so sovereign that He gives us freedom to choose. He does not always get His way with nations and men. He calls those who will work with Him. Greater than a god who controls all the choices of all people is the God who still accomplishes His purposes by willing co-workers. The ones who follow His Son are the ones He is using to change lives. The ones who are praying, "Thy kingdom come," and are bringing the kingdom near by the manner of their lives are the ones He is using to change the world.

## 10-13
### God Is Not Insecure
The One who planted the trees in the Garden of Eden gave humankind a choice. He is not insecure about our freedom. He is kind and patient with those who may be upset with Him. He is not unsettled when we get it wrong. He is not wringing His hands. He patiently keeps coming back by overtures of inviting grace. He seeks for co-laborers who will help Him. "And I sought for a man among them who should build up the wall and stand in the breach before me for the land, that I should not destroy it, but I found none." (Ezekiel 22:30 ESV).

## 10-14
### Jesus Did Not Say
The things Jesus did not say to the disciples after the resurrection: "You forsook me." "You denied me." "You did not pray with me". Instead He spoke peace to

them. It was peace that had an unasked-for forgiveness in it. It was peace driven by grace. It was peace without condemnation. It was not just spoken shalom; it was reinforced when He gave them the breath of the Spirit. There is something here that we disciples must learn if we would spread His peace. Giving peace to others in the same way Jesus gave peace to us is the core of being a true peacemaker.

"That Sunday evening the disciples were meeting behind locked doors because they were afraid of the Jewish leaders. Suddenly, Jesus was standing there among them! 'Peace be with you,' he said." John 20:19 (NLT)

## 10-15
### When God Goes Looking
When the Lord has a job to do He goes looking for a person. He found a righteous man in Noah. He found a walking partner in a man named Enoch. He found an Abraham and sent him out of a land of many gods, to take Him on a journey where He could reveal Himself as One. With him, He established a covenant. He went looking for the shepherd Moses to liberate the oppressed covenant people. He went calling in the temple in the middle of the night to select a boy named Samuel. He found Him a king in David, and chose to be one of his descendants. He looked for a watchman and could not find one. He found a godly couple to parent John the Baptizer. He found a willing Mary and Joseph to give earthly nurture to His Son. He decided on a woman to be the first evangel of the Resurrection, looking past eleven men. He went looking for a preacher to the Gentiles and found him in the unlikely persecutor named Saul. There are thousands more that He found to work with Him throughout biblical history. God is still looking, and calling. He is looking for you to be His willing servant. He can do more through you than you ever dreamed. Heed the call. Be His walking partner also.

"God looks down from heaven on the children of man to see if there are any who understand, who seek after God." Psalm 53:2 (ESV)


## 10-16
### Getting To Know God
An atheist says that there is no God. A practical atheist acts as if there is no God. But can it be that there is another kind of atheist who has constructed a

god that does not exist because he will not accept the One who is revealed? Can it be that there are atheists who are really not atheists, but they have merely rejected the God that some well-meaning person has misrepresented Him to be? We believe that God reveals Himself. Without this we could not know Him. Christians believe that God has made Himself known in Jesus of Nazareth. People need to know Jesus. Jesus is all about getting to know our Father God.

Jesus said, "If you have seen me, you have seen the Father" (John 14:9).

## 10-17
### God Whispers
Elijah heard some loud noises in the opening of a cave, but it was not God speaking. He finally heard God in a whisper (1 Kings 19:11-12). We are surrounded with lots of noise. Noises of the world keep us from hearing the whispering voice. The only way we can hear the voice that whispers is to be totally quiet. Distracting noises must be silenced. Tune out the world's racket. God is not given over to yelling. He does whisper though.

"But the LORD is in His holy temple. Let all the earth be silent before Him." Habakkuk 2:20 (NASB)

## 10-18
### Come Home
The God who is enthroned in Heaven desires to be enthroned in your heart. He who rides the clouds, paints the sunrise and sunset, hung the stars, holds the waters in the palm of His hand and raised the mountains above the waters, longs for you. He who was a friend of Abraham wants to be your friend. He who walked with Enoch wants to walk with you. He who gave His Child to you wants you to be His child. The Father's arms are open. He is your Home. Come home! Oh sinner, come home!

"And he arose and came to his father. But while he was still a long way off, his father saw him and felt compassion, and ran and embraced him and kissed him. And the son said to him, 'Father, I have sinned against heaven and before you. I am no longer worthy to be called your son.' But the father said to his servants, 'Bring quickly the best robe, and put it on him, and put a ring on his hand, and shoes on his feet. And bring the fattened calf and kill it, and let us eat and celebrate.'" Luke 15:20-23 (ESV)

## 10-19
### Jesus Messiah
We have come to think that Christ is the last name of Jesus. No! Christ means Messiah, anointed one, long promised descendent of David, king of the Kingdom of God (i.e. God's Government) and Lord of the whole earth. He reigns even as we speak at the right hand of God. As Christians this must totally change our worldview. Colossians 3 tells us how we as Kingdom citizens should live in this world, given the reality of our enthroned Messiah.

"Therefore if you have been raised up with Messiah, keep seeking the things above, where Messiah is, seated at the right hand of God. Set your mind on the things above, not on the things that are on earth." Colossians 3:1-2

## 10-20
### Insulting Words
You can kill with more than a gun. You can do it with words. Hate is a failure to love our neighbors. (I don't think we will be erecting Jesus' commandments on murder, nor the one on adultery in the halls of government. It would embarrass the politicians). We like Moses' words, without Jesus' profound commentary and in-depth interpretation. Disrespectful-insulting-mocking-shameful name calling: like idiot, zero, stupid, ignorant, retard, dummy, good-for-nothing, etc., all are violations of the commandment, "You shall not murder." The opposite of murder is to love, honor and respect all folks with whom your life intersects.

"You have heard that it was said to those of ancient times, 'You shall not murder'; and 'whoever murders shall be liable to judgment.' But I say to you that if you are angry with a brother or sister, you will be liable to judgment; and if you insult a brother or sister, you will be liable to the council; and if you say, 'You fool,' you will be liable to the hell of fire." Matthew 5:21-22 (NRSV)

## 10-21
### God Models His Own Commands
The God revealed in Jesus of Nazareth does not ask us to do anything He has not already done. There is no sacrifice you make that He has not made. He who

said, "Take up your cross" already took up His. He went the second mile. He turned the other cheek. He loved His enemies. He forgave those who mistreated Him. How about the Golden Rule? "As you would that others do unto you, do also to them." Well, He does that too! He does not force Himself on us. That is contrary to His nature of love. He gives us space and time. He is the Gentleman who always gives us respect and love. The Holy Trinity lives in a community of self-giving love. The way God, as Trinity, behaves with God is the way we are to behave with each other.

## 10-22
### What A Wonder!
The God who paints the sunrise and sunsets has time to love me. The Creator of all things is active in my heart and life. The God of Abraham, Isaac and Israel is the One who also walks with me. The God who raised our Lord Jesus from the dead has sent His Spirit to live in my heart and keeps raising me up. The One who sustained and guided a nation across 40 years of wilderness is intimately involved in my wilderness experience. What a wonder! He Loves Me!

## 10-23
### Words Create Worlds
The world was created by words. Everything that is was spoken into existence by One Who is called Word. We also create worlds by words; the words we speak to others and the words we speak to ourselves create or demolish. Nations are built by words and brought down by them. Worlds of fear and anxiety are created by words. Words lead us to reality or they create false realities. Words drive and destroy dreams. Words shape heroes and villains. They create order or chaos. Words are behind the great turning points of history. The words of the gospel are ultimately intended for new creation. Participate!

"By faith we understand that the worlds were prepared by the word of God, so that what is seen was not made out of things which are visible" (Hebrews 11:3 NASB). "The words that I have spoken to you are spirit and life" (John 6:63).

## 10-24
### When The Kingdom Comes
The kingdom is here and it will come. When it comes in its fullness:

There will be no racism, classism, elitism, sexism or cronyism.
There will be no "us" and "them".
There will be no divisions, hatreds, covetousness, domination or oppression.
There will be no rich and poor. There will be no haves and have nots.
There will be no injustice, unrighteousness, wickedness, iniquity.
There will be no worship in the absence of compassion and righteousness.
There will be no singing in the absence of justice.
If that is the way it is going to be then; it needs to begin now with everyone who names the name of the Lord.

"Take away from Me the noise of your songs, For I will not hear the melody of your stringed instruments. But let justice run down like water, And righteousness like a mighty stream." Amos 5:23-24 (NKJV)

## 10-25
### Submission
Some religious groups promote a rigid submission to their adherents, others go further and insist on submission from non-adherents. Christianity teaches submission to a God who submits. God reconciled the world through a path of submission. He submitted to being human; He even submitted Himself to His enemies who nailed Him to a cross. He submissively knocks at the door of the human will awaiting admission. There is mutual submission in the Trinity. The NT teaches mutual submission in the Christian Community and marriage. Our salvation comes in submitting to the God who submitted to incarnation and the cross. Who could not love to submit to a God like that? We fail to submit because we want to be god. In so doing we do not become godly, but ungodly; the real God is not like that. A life of submission to Him is the path to salvation, happiness and glory. We are only kidding ourselves if we think salvation is something else.

"God is opposed to the proud, but gives grace to the humble." Submit therefore to God...Draw near to God and He will draw near to you...Humble yourselves in the presence of the Lord, and He will exalt you." James 4:6-10 (NASB)

## 10-26
### The Un-box-able God
One of the hardest things we have to do is let go of bad teaching about God and the Christian faith; it is so deeply entrenched in our psyche with our vested

interest in it, that we can't turn it loose. Our personal views of the faith evolves over time. When the Word Himself leads us we make progress. We can never encapsulate in our minds the greatness of Truth, but we can certainly allow our horizons to expand and our understanding to deepen. The renewal of our mind includes deeper knowledge, changing our attitudes, and putting Truth into practice. Let the Lord break your old molds and set you on a blessed journey of discovery of the un-box-able God.

"Of LORD our Lord, how excellent is thy name in all the earth! who hast set thy glory above the heavens." Psalm 8:1 (KJV)

## 10-27
### Let It Shine
The darker the night the brighter the stars. Night cannot put out the Light. A candle shows brighter when it is pitch black. Quit blaming the dark for the problems of the world. We have become pros at cursing the darkness. We have hidden our lights under our agendas. We have preached fear, when we should have been preaching hope. We have become too anemic for a radical gospel. Our Light is Christ in us. The staff that holds the light up is our obedient witness. The thing that compels us to carry it is love.

"In him was life, and the life was the light of men. The light shines in the darkness, and the darkness has not overcome it." John 1:4-5 (ESV)

## 10-28
### Hearing god Or Hearing God
Humankind have a way of hearing a god who is not God commanding them. They say it is god, but it is not God. This god is one constructed by personal likes, dislikes, prejudices and fears, as well as by covetousness, competition and conquest. This god can "command" some horrific things. This god, we too often hear speak, is ourselves. This god is much into setting "us" against "them"; this god wants "us" to make war with "them", discredit "them", demonize "them" and defeat "them" and he is always on our side. The real God commands us to love enemies, to feed and clothe them, to supply them with water, to invite them in, welcome them as equals into a Kingdom of redeemed sinners, to sit at the same table with them, and to pass them peace at a sacramental meal.

"And I tell you this, that many Gentiles will come from all over the world—from east and west—and sit down with Abraham, Isaac, and Jacob at the feast in the Kingdom of Heaven." Matthew 8:11 (NLT)

## 10-29
### Love Rescues
Egypt was salvation for Israel through the slavery of Joseph. The nation was fed and favored through the years of intense famine. 400-plus years later Egypt had become a brutal place of slavery. The God who loved them into Egypt now loved them out of Egypt. The God who loved them through the wilderness "on eagle wings" loved them through the Jordan to the land of covenant. "God is Love!" did not start in the NT; through Jesus Messiah it was revealed that rescuing love had always been the essence of His Father.

## 10-30
### Washing Feet
When Jesus washed the disciples feet He asked them, "Do you know what I have done?" —meaning— "Do you know why I have done this?" It was surely bigger than an act to be enshrined as a sacrament. It was a message to bickering disciples who wanted to be greater than each other. It is still a message to our private thoughts where we think of ourselves as better than our peers. It is a message that reminds us that our real assignment is to serve each other, and "in lowliness of mind let each esteem others better than themselves" (Philippians 2:3). I think we know what it means, but I fear we have not yet put it into a comprehensive way of life.

## 10-31
### Warm God's Heart
Nations use terror to drive out or subdue indigenous people in their expansion. We have often attributed victory after such brutal conquest to our tribal god. The Father of Jesus is not angry at the people your nation is angry about. We lift our kind of people above the other peoples of our world. God is the Father of all of them. He loves them. He wants to bless them. Abba wants all of His children to get along in the world. Nothing warms the heart of parents like seeing their children loving on, and doing good things for each other. It is like no other good

feeling that parents have. Why don't we just start warming the heart of our Father!

Everyone who believes that Jesus is the Christ is born of God, and everyone who loves the father loves his child as well. This is how we know that we love the children of God: by loving God and carrying out his commands." 1 John 5:1-2 (NIV)

## 11-1
### Collective Comprehension
There is a collective comprehension that can be found only in the congregation of believers. Consider these words, "...May be able to comprehend with all the saints what is the breadth and length and height and depth, and to know the love of Christ which surpasses knowledge, that you may be filled up to all the fullness of God" (Ephesians 3:18-19 NASB). We know better together than we can know individually. The church is the school of the Spirit. He is the Spirit of our Teacher; He is the Spirit of Truth Who makes truth clear. Private interpretations can get us away from the truths that the church has always believed (2 Peter 1:20). The Spirit working in the body is essential for a knowing "which surpasses knowledge".

## 11-2
### Low Times
Life brings with it high times and low times. We tend to make these times a barometer of our relationship with God. We do not want to make that mistake. This is not a measure of God's blessings or non-blessing. Emotions, body chemistry, illness, life events, circumstances and many more things fuel highs and lows. The Spirit of God is not a puppet Who is pulled around by our highs and lows. God is with us at all times. His love assures that our Shepherd is very near at those times when we struggle.

"He became their Savior. In all their troubles, he was troubled, too. He didn't send someone else to help them. He did it himself, in person. Out of his own love and pity he redeemed them. He rescued them and carried them along for a long, long time." Isaiah 63:8b-9 (MSG)

## 11-3
### He Is Lord
The Roman empire had brought prosperity to the world. A strong military kept their enemies at bay. Lots of folks did not want to say anything against it. They went along to get along, even if they would need to say, "Caesar is Lord". They could continue to buy and sell in the markets bringing prosperity, after all, they had to feed their families. There was a heavy price to saying, "Caesar is not Lord; Jesus is Lord." Those early Christians did not try to rationalize the statement, "Jesus is Lord" as their private spirituality in a compartment, while going along with an evil system. They lived and confessed, "Jesus is Lord" to persecution and sometimes death. It was the cost of living, believing and confessing it.

"If you confess with your lips that Jesus is Lord and believe in your heart that God raised him from the dead, you will be saved...For there is no distinction between Jew and Greek; the same Lord is Lord of all and is generous to all who call on him." Romans 10:9, 12 (NRSV)

## 11-4
### Pray for the Persecuted Church
Bearing the cross was about suffering and death for the early Christians. Many ended up: on a Roman cross, losing their jobs and homes, in an arena of lions, burned at the stake, fried in oil, and a thousand tortures imagined from diabolical minds. It is still that for some of our brothers and sisters in regions of persecution. Pray for them to stand firm, persevere, and for their protection. They are our brothers and sisters. In that Great Day they will shine as the stars of the morning. We will not be worthy to stand alongside them.

"Others were tortured and refused to be released, so that they might gain a better resurrection. Some faced jeers and flogging, while still others were chained and put in prison. They were stoned; they were sawed in two; they were put to death by the sword. They went about in sheepskins and goatskins, destitute, persecuted and mistreated-- the world was not worthy of them. They wandered in deserts and mountains, and in caves and holes in the ground." Hebrews 11:35b-38 (NIV)

## 11-5
### Non-Forcing Love
A family member is killed. A spouse wants a divorce. A loved one is hooked on drugs. A partner ruins a business with an irrational choice. Cancer comes from someone's bad environmental choices. A thousand other things could be listed of what persons in our network of family and friends can do that drastically affect us. This can hit us very hard. We pray. Sometimes the prayers go unanswered. Why do these things happen? God gives us freedom; God is love, the love of God does not permit Him to force the other person to do the right thing. Love can persuade, but love never forces. God lives with that. We have to live with that. Just remember, the One who had friends to forsake Him, false witnesses to speak against Him, and endured an evil cross, is the very One Who walks with us to mature us in our troubles.

"Love does not insist on its own way". 1 Corinthians 13:5 (ESV)


## 11-6
### Disappointment With God
Sometimes we are disappointed with God, because we expected Him to act in a way He did not. We had visualized an answer to prayer that would come in a certain way, or in a certain time; it did not. We become hurt with the Father! But wait! The problem here is not with God, but us. We wanted Him to control the situation, and He did not. We have always said, "God is in control," but He did not exercise "control". The situation got worse. The persons we wanted Him to change became meaner. God is very much into persuading and loving and not into forcing and controlling. When we are disappointed with God, we need to pause and ask ourselves this question: "Have I constructed a God in my mind and my theology who does not exist?" Let God be Who He is!

"God said to Moses, 'I AM WHO I AM'...{*In Hebrew it means, "I WILL BE WHO I WILL BE."*} 'This is My name forever, and this is My memorial-name to all generations'" Ex 3:14a, 15b (NASB).


## 11-7
### Sleeping Through A Revolution
The legendary Rip Van Winkle slept through a revolution that kept everyone else awake at night. Sleeping through a revolution does not prevent it from carrying

you along and waking you up in another place and time. It is easier to sleep than to engage. The church is in such a time where cultural forces are taking us somewhere else. Some want to load us up on a train to transport us back to the time before the revolution. Some see revival's goal being to take us back to that ideal time, some golden age. We do need revival; we do need our spirits revived and revitalized to serve this present age. We need the Holy Spirit to fill and empower us for today. We need to be wide awake to where the Spirit is carrying us now. His train never goes back. All Aboard!

"He who has ears to hear, let him hear what the Spirit is saying to the churches" (Revelation 2 & 3).

## 11-8
### The Seeker Of Sinners
Adam's sin made him hide from God, but God's reaction is to go searching for Adam; He did not go the other way. God does not flee from sinners; He runs toward them. He refuses separation, preferring rather reunion and restoration of the relationship. Jesus demonstrated this kind of Father when He went to parties with and for sinners. He intentionally spent time with sinners. How are we doing on this aspect of being Christlike?

"For the Son of Man came to seek and to save what was lost." Luke 19:10 (NIV)

## 11-9
### Danger Of The Mundane
Life can be mundane. The repetition of recurring tasks can dull our spiritual senses. It can get us in a place where we retreat from active engagement with those around us. We must not let it shut out those in need of ministry. The mundane can also affect our movements toward God. Don't set up camp there. Renew your covenant. Let the Spirit refresh you.

"Jesus said, 'You're tied down to the mundane; I'm in touch with what is beyond your horizons. You live in terms of what you see and touch. I'm living on other terms. I told you that you were missing God in all this. You're at a dead end. If you won't believe I am who I say I am, you're at the dead end of sins. You're missing God in your lives.'" John 8:23-24 (MSG)

## 11-10
### The Cast-down Soul
"Why are you cast down, O my soul, and why are you disquieted within me? Hope in God; for I shall again praise him, my help and my God" (Psalm 42:5-6a NRSV).   Sometimes we ask ourselves, "WHY?", but no answer comes. Sometimes we may know the source of the pain and sometimes we may never know, but in our darkness and pain we turn to the Lord. We believe something; we trust Someone beyond our pain. We know He is our Helper; therefore, we praise Him.

## 11-11
### We Stand In Christ
Adam sinned and fell. Humans still sin and still fall. "Death passed from Adam to all in that all sinned" (Romans 5:12). The Tree of Life was not enough for Adam. This Tree was a type of Him Who was to come. Adam walked away from it, and we have walked away from it. Every time we fail to follow the teachings of Jesus we fall, because we are walking away from the Tree of Life. Following Him and His teaching brings the Life He came to give us. When we live in solidarity with Him we will stand.

"Therefore, just as through one man sin entered into the world, and death through sin, and so death spread to all men, because all sinned." Romans 5:12 (NASB)

## 11-12
### The Things That Hold Us
John Wimber, in "Spirit Song," used the following words. "Oh, let him have the things that hold you, and his Spirit, like a dove, Will descend upon your life and make you whole." We tend not to think about the things that hold us. We hold things or things hold us. If they hold us, then they hamper our spiritual growth. They keep us in cages when we were meant to fly. They hold us in dark caves where we cannot see the great vistas all around us. Let Jesus have the things that hold you and you can become whole and spiritually healthy.

## 11-13
### The Submission of Christ
"For to be sure, he was crucified in weakness" (2 Corinthians 13:4a NIV). This is the scandal of the Messiah being crucified. He submitted to a Roman execution, corrupt Jewish leaders, to the mob, and "like a lamb led to slaughter He opened not his mouth" (Isaiah 53:7). He submitted in weakness to the full weight of human evil being poured out on Him. It was in this paradoxical way that He was also submitting to His Father and the impassable cup. It was that submission that became the pattern for His followers as they submitted to persecution in the spirit of Christ. Out of this submission comes victory, out of this weakness comes power, out of this dying comes resurrection, out of this despair comes hope, and out of this evil comes good. We know that all things come out for the good to those who follow the Lamb, for we have seen the cross and we have seen the empty tomb.

"For to be sure, he was crucified in weakness, yet he lives by God's power. Likewise, we are weak in him, yet by God's power we will live with him to serve you." 2 Corinthians 13:4 (NIV)

## 11-14
### Pure Joy!?
"Consider it pure joy, my brothers, whenever you face trials of many kinds, because you know that the testing of your faith develops perseverance. Perseverance must finish its work so that you may be mature and complete, not lacking anything" (James 1:2-4 NIV). Consider facing trials as pure joy? Paradox! Counterintuitive! We want only a joy that elates us; there is a joy that is not centered in pleasure. Are we there yet? One thing for sure, complaining and griping indicate that we are not. Fretting does not get us there. How do we get there? We get there by surrendering the trials and knowing that the things we are wanting to protest are the very things that are shaping us like our tried and tested Lord.

## 11-15
### The Lord Is Our Life
Israel was admonished to choose life over death and blessing over the curse (Deuteronomy 27-30). What we miss in this is that the Lord is our life as we obey His voice and hold fast to Him. "Choose life, that you and your offspring may live,

loving the LORD your God, obeying his voice and holding fast to him, for he is your life" (Deuteronomy 30:19b-20a ESV). In Him is life; in Christ we have life. Faith is holding fast to Him. Obeying His voice is an expression of true faith.

"When Christ, who is our life, is revealed, then you also will be revealed with Him in glory." Colossians 3:4 (NASB)

## 11-16
### Turning Point
The blind man had spent his life asking for coins, but his life was forever changed when he asked Jesus for mercy. Too many spend their lives making a living and never live. They come to the end of their lives and realize that it was for naught. Jesus becomes for all who call on Him a turning point when life can start in a whole new direction. In that moment we receive our sight, the lost is found and the chained are free.

"Then they came to Jericho. And as He was leaving Jericho with His disciples and a large crowd, a blind beggar named Bartimaeus, the son of Timaeus, was sitting by the road. When he heard that it was Jesus the Nazarene, he began to cry out and say, 'Jesus, Son of David, have mercy on me!'" Mark 10:46-47 (NASB)

## 11-17
### The Relationship Requires It
There are some things that cannot be separated in the NT, though we try: God's forgiveness of us and our forgiving others, nor His love for us and our love for others, nor His mercy for us and being just that merciful to those around us, nor His overflowing grace and our giving grace. These things always go together: Understanding and appreciating His forgiveness of us requires that we forgive; when His unconditional love has finally penetrated our hearts, mind and soul, we know to maintain the relationship we have to give love away; how can we withhold mercy from another when it has been so freely given to us? The inability to give grace is a sure sign that we have not yet fully received it ourselves. Freely we have received, and freely we give. The receiving must be connected to the giving in this relationship of God, you and others. What we keep we lose; what we give away we possess. It can never be just about you

and God. It always involves others. Forgiveness, love, mercy and grace is just how it works with the Father and His children.

Father, free us from the illusion that we have Your gifts when we hoard them. Teach us to give away what You give us so we will bear Your DNA, proving that You are our Father. Amen!

## 11-18
### What We Are
In our early Christian immaturity we thought that the will of God meant to be in the exact place God wanted us to be as well as being there with the right mate. We finally learned that it is much bigger than that. The will of God is more about who we are than where we are. The will of God is that we love and forgive, show mercy and kindness, be a peacemaker and a servant. We are to pursue the divine likeness as the goal of our relationship with Him. The will of God is about holiness as Christlikeness.

"The world is passing away, and also its lusts; but the one who does the will of God lives forever." 1 John 2:17 (NASB)

## 11-19
### Precious Connections
Some of the greatest shaping of my life has been the positive influences of brothers and sisters in the church network. It has been more than fellowship, though I love the ties that bind us. It is being connected with fellow believers that have modeled Christlikeness in the tough and trying places of life. They have encouraged me when I was down. They have shown me Jesus in inspiring ways. We have borne each others' griefs and burdens and we have shared each others' joys and triumphs. The Lord of the Church calls us to be Jesus to each other.

"Having so fond an affection for you, we were well-pleased to impart to you not only the gospel of God but also our own lives, because you had become very dear to us." 1 Thessalonians 2:8 (NASB)

## 11-20
### Don't Miss Your Cross
Don't run out of time before you die; die on the cross before you run out of time. Jesus taught us that we cannot live until we die. There is no resurrection until there has been a death. There is no rising without going down. There is no blossoming of self until there is a denying of self. A kernel of wheat dies that it might live; our deaths become a germination to a new form. There is no going higher until we have gone lower. There is no living in the highest sense of the word without the cross.

"If anyone wishes to come after Me, he must deny himself, and take up his cross daily and follow Me." Luke 9:23 (NASB)


## 11-21
### Life Will Test Our Love
The privileged have their own particular set of complaints that the poor cannot relate to nor even comprehend. We complain about goods and services not being the best, when sometimes the poor have none of the things of which we complain. Jesus said, "The poor you always have with you"; He certainly did not mean we can sigh and say, "Oh, well!" The truth is, they are always with us to test our compassion, the test of giving to others the gifts and graciousness we have received from God. He came to us in our poverty with the gifts of grace. If we can give it away, it is pretty good evidence that we have received it.


## 11-22
### We Do Know
"Simon Peter replied, 'You are the Messiah, the Son of the living God'" Matthew 16:16). This is the great confession. It was understood that the Messiah would be the Son of David, but when He came it was also revealed that Messiah was the Son of God. David's son was David's Lord (Psalm 110:1); He was before David, but descended from him. The Son then is the Cosmic Christ who has always been at the Father's right hand. Our great confession comes not from flesh and blood's mere human reasoning, but comes out of a deep Spirit-inspired knowing. The Father delights in revealing Messiah by His Spirit to our spirit.

"Simon Peter replied, 'You are the Christ, the Son of the living God.' And Jesus answered him, 'Blessed are you, Simon Bar-Jonah! For flesh and blood has not revealed this to you, but my Father who is in heaven.'" Matthew 16:16-17

## 11-23
### Follow The Lamb
Follow the Lamb? We prefer to follow a lion. Mr. Lion gets our vote. We want someone who is strong, commanding and triumphant who will devour our enemies. We forget that Satan is a roaring lion seeking whom he may devour. Following the Lamb to His sacrificial death, who dies in weakness and not in power, just does not stir us to wave our flag. Following Him by carrying our cross means we go willingly to our own dying. Following the Lamb means that we will live in this world in lamb ways and not in lion ways.

"If anyone serves Me, he must follow Me; and where I am, there My servant will be also; if anyone serves Me, the Father will honor him." John 12:26 (NASB)

## 11-24
### Healing And Wholeness
Sin seen in relationship to the law is a transgression to be punished and an action that needs forgiveness. Sin seen as sickness points us to the need to be healed from a disease that needs a radical cure. Sin is a deep brokenness at the core of our being. It needs a physician, even the Great Physician. The answer to sin's sickness is spiritual health and wholeness. There is a balm in Gilead; there is a physician there, "so that the health of His people can be restored" (Jeremiah 8:22).

Father, when we view persons in the grip of sin, help us not to think about how badly they need to be punished, but rather how much they need to be healed. Amen!

## 11-25
### Jesus Endured The Cross
I don't like crosses. They are painful. Jesus also "endured the cross, despising the shame." He not only endured it, He embraced it. It was necessary to complete His race, so He kept on running. That's your example. That's my

example. He will be there to help us; we will not have to do it alone. The cross is necessary for us to complete our race also.

"Therefore, since we have so great a cloud of witnesses surrounding us, let us also lay aside every encumbrance and the sin which so easily entangles us, and let us run with endurance the race that is set before us, fixing our eyes on Jesus, the author and perfecter of faith, who for the joy set before Him endured the cross, despising the shame, and has sat down at the right hand of the throne of God." Hebrews 12:1-2 (NASB)

## 11-26
### Gratitude, A Way Of Life
Make thanksgiving a way of life and not just an annual event. Make thanksgiving a part of everyday of your life. Look around you; there are many persons to whom you can say thank you. Keep up the habit of thanksgiving until it flows from your heart as a genuine gratitude. Cultivate a heart of overflowing gratitude to the Lord for His manifold blessings. Gratitude as a way of life will make your burdens lighter and your problems less overwhelming.

"Rejoice always; pray without ceasing; in everything give thanks; for this is God's will for you in Christ Jesus." 1 Thessalonians 5:16-18 (NASB)

## 11-27
### Overspending
Why do we spend more than we earn? Why do we create debt that we can't afford? Is it rooted in covetousness? Is it an unwillingness to be content with what we have? Is it a desire to have all the things that others have, though we have not yet earned enough to have them? Is it about immediate gratification where the virtues of discipline, patience and delayed gratification are despised? Is it about competition and status? Is it about wrongful pride? Is it not a spiritual problem? Does it not call for repentance? Does it not call for developing disciplines that will produce a character change?

"Take heed and beware of covetousness, for one's life does not consist in the abundance of the things he possesses." Luke 12:15

## 11-28
### The spirit of antichrist
The spirit of antichrist is that which denies the incarnation; it is to deny that the eternal Christ came in the flesh of Jesus of Nazareth (1 John 4:2-3). It is to deny that there is a perfect oneness of Father and Son in Jesus Messiah. God the Father declared physical matter good in the creation, He reaffirmed it when His Son came in flesh. To call the physical world evil is an attack on the Creator. To believe that only the spiritual is good is a grave error. Science itself shows us that matter and energy are really one. This world is created and sustained by the Energy of God. The New Testament says that the Name of that "Energy" is Jesus Messiah. Jesus Messiah is the grand Mystery of the universe. If we have come to know Him, we have come to know the Father. If we embrace Him, we are embracing the Father. Now let us worship!

"By this you know the Spirit of God: every spirit that confesses that Jesus Christ has come in the flesh is from God, and every spirit that does not confess Jesus is not from God. This is the spirit of the antichrist, which you heard was coming and now is in the world already" (1 John 4:2-3 ESV). "Who is the liar but he who denies that Jesus is the Christ? This is the antichrist, he who denies the Father and the Son. No one who denies the Son has the Father. Whoever confesses the Son has the Father also" (1 John 2:22-23 ESV).

## 11-29
### Jesus Will Return
Jesus will come back again. The angels promised it. The apostles proclaimed it. The creeds declare it. A broken world needs it. He will come to restore all things; He will make all things new. The One who created the universe will make a new creation wherein dwells righteousness. Heaven and earth will become one. Pain and sickness will be gone (Revelation 21). Darkness and death will be banished by Light and Life. The deepest longings of our soul will be filled with the peaceful rest of knowing we are finally home with our Lord.

"When he had said this, as they were watching, he was lifted up, and a cloud took him out of their sight. While he was going and they were gazing up toward heaven, suddenly two men in white robes stood by them. They said, 'Men of Galilee, why do you stand looking up toward heaven? This Jesus, who has been taken up from you into heaven, will come in the same way as you saw him go into heaven.'" Acts 1:9-11 (NRSV)

**11-30**
**Creator-Shepherd**
"Know ye that the LORD he is God: it is he that hath made us, and not we ourselves; we are his people, and the sheep of his pasture" (Psalm 100:3 KJV). The Lord is our Creator and He is also our Shepherd. All people are His creation. He loves them all. They are His people. He longs to shepherd us. He wants to keep leading us to the green pastures He has provided. A shepherd means feeder of sheep; He feeds us with Himself. He is "the Bread that came down from heaven." Our spirits need this spiritual food for life.

"Those who eat my flesh and drink my blood abide in me, and I in them...When many of his disciples heard it, they said, 'This teaching is difficult; who can accept it?' But Jesus, being aware that his disciples were complaining about it, said to them, 'Does this offend you? It is the spirit that gives life; the flesh is useless. The words that I have spoken to you are spirit and life." John 6:56, 61-63 (NRSV)

**12-1**
**Being Different (1)**
Nicodemas thought Jesus meant "born again"; Jesus clarified that He meant "born from above" (John 3:1-8). Being "born from above" truly makes our lives different in this world "below". Too many who claim to be "born again" Christians look no different that those around them. "Born from above" is a transformation accomplished by the Spirit. Those having been born of the Spirit manifest the fruit of the Spirit from their lives. "But the fruit of the Spirit is love, joy, peace, patience, kindness, goodness, faithfulness, gentleness, self-control" (Galatians 5:22-23a NASB).

"Jesus answered him, 'Very truly, I tell you, no one can see the kingdom of God without being born from above." John 3:3 (NRSV)

**12-2**
**Being Different (2)**
Those "born from above" live the Golden Rule. They are not harsh. Love for God and others is truly shaping their lives, their actions and their reactions. "Love is patient; love is kind; love is not envious or boastful or arrogant or rude. It does not insist on its own way; it is not irritable or resentful; it does not rejoice in

wrongdoing, but rejoices in the truth. It bears all things, believes all things, hopes all things, endures all things" (1 Corinthians 13:4-7 NRSV). God is love and thus His Spirit is love. "Born from above" means the Spirit by which we are born is ever transforming us to look like our Father who is love!

Jesus answered him, "Very truly, I tell you, no one can see the kingdom of God without being born from above." John 3:3 (NRSV)

## 12-3
### Being Different (3)

"Jesus answered him, 'Very truly, I tell you, no one can see the kingdom of God without being born from above'" (John 3:3 NRSV). Do you know what we have left out of that verse in our haste to promote the new birth? It is the "kingdom of God" — seeing the kingdom — having a vision of the government of God — living in the kingdom as our primary place of being — not caught up with the governments of this world, but seeking to live out the government of God, which invites all to become citizens of the Kingdom. Being "born from above", seeing the Kingdom, has huge implications about how we live in a political world! Is not Jesus saying that the goal of being "born from above" is to "see the Kingdom"? It is here even now! See it! Live in it! Live by its values!

## 12-4
### Being Different (4)

"But just as he who called you is holy, so be holy in all you do; for it is written: 'Be holy, because I am holy'" (1 Peter 1:15-16 NIV). We usually say that "holy" means to be "set apart"; it also means "different". God is different than any other being. He is in a category by Himself. For us to be "holy" means that we are to live out the nature and likeness of God as His image-bearers in the world. Jesus quoted "be holy" as "be perfect". "Therefore you are to be perfect, as your heavenly Father is perfect." The context (Matthew 5:43-48) tells us that "perfect" means that we are to love like our Father loves. Thus "being different" as God is different means indiscriminate love for all, including our enemies. That's what "born from above" looks like.

## 12-5
### Jesus' Best Man
John the Baptist's life pointed inexplicably and unwaveringly to Jesus. He said, "Behold the Lamb of God who takes away the sin of the world." He saw himself as the "friend of the bridegroom" who "rejoices greatly at the bridegroom's voice." His own voice said, "I am the voice of one crying out in the wilderness, 'Make straight the way of the Lord,' as the prophet Isaiah said'" (John 1:23 NRSV). He loved it that Jesus "must increase, but I must decrease" (John 3:30). He rejoiced when his numbers went down. He was not into being somebody great, with a great career and a great following. He was all about Jesus. He wanted to be in the background and Jesus in the foreground. Not a bad example to follow.

"They came to John and said to him, "Rabbi, the one who was with you across the Jordan, to whom you testified, here he is baptizing, and all are going to him." John answered, "No one can receive anything except what has been given from heaven. You yourselves are my witnesses that I said, 'I am not the Messiah, but I have been sent ahead of him.' He who has the bride is the bridegroom. The friend of the bridegroom, who stands and hears him, rejoices greatly at the bridegroom's voice. For this reason my joy has been fulfilled. He must increase, but I must decrease." John 3:26-30 (NRSV)

## 12-6
### Our Encouraging Father
Our Father is an encourager. He wants no one to fail. It is not His desire or will for anyone to perish. He wills no one's failure. He wants us to succeed. He cheers from the sidelines. He sent His Son to show us how to run the race. He sent His Spirit to enable us to succeed. His love never stops; it never gives up; it is eternally unending. Take a longer look at your Father. See His kind eyes. Hear His encouraging words.

"If God is for us, who can be against us?...."For I am sure that neither death nor life, nor angels nor rulers, nor things present nor things to come, nor powers, nor height nor depth, nor anything else in all creation, will be able to separate us from the love of God in Christ Jesus our Lord." Romans 8:31b, 38-39 (ESV)

## 12-7
### Build A Life
You can't build a life on what you are against. What we are opposed to is a sad way to state our "faith". "Now faith is the assurance of things hoped for, the conviction of things not seen" (Hebrews 11:1 ESV). The Apostles' Creed states what we believe, as does the Nicene Creed. Faith believes that God has raised from the dead our Lord Jesus Christ and that His resurrection has changed our lives and our future. You can build your life on that, for sure.

The Apostles' Creed:
I believe in God the Father, Almighty, Maker of heaven and earth: And in Jesus Christ, his only begotten Son, our Lord: Who was conceived by the Holy Spirit, born of the Virgin Mary: Suffered under Pontius Pilate; was crucified, dead and buried: He descended into hades: The third day he rose again from the dead:
He ascended into heaven, and sits at the right hand of God the Father Almighty: From thence he shall come to judge the quick and the dead: I believe in the Holy Spirit: I believe in the holy catholic church: the communion of saints: The forgiveness of sins: The resurrection of the body: And the life everlasting. Amen.

## 12-8
### Faith And Faithfulness
Faith expresses itself by its works, what it does, how it obeys, how it serves, and how it loves. {"Faith works by love" (Gal 5:6). "Faith without works is dead" (James 2:14-26).} These show the presence of faith. When these are present over the days of our lives, it is called faithfulness. May our faith never shrink, but always grow toward mature faith.

Father, we desire to live a life full of faith, confidence and trust in you. May we manifest our faith by works of love, acts of service, and from-the-heart obedience. Amen!

## 12-9
### No Going Back
"Demas, in love with this present world, has deserted me and gone to Thessalonica" (2 Timothy 4:10a NRSV). Oh, the pain of Paul's words! Going back is in the realm of our choice. Is not "love of this present world" going back within itself? (1 John 2:15-17). I do not want to go back. The promises of this

world are a mirage. It will betray my Lord. It will change my story for the worse. It will betray those who follow me. It will be walking away from the "age to come" to only embrace this "present age". It is a denial that the better Kingdom has come. Going back would mean that I regret having put my hands to the plow (Luke 9:62). "The world behind me, the cross before me; no turning back, no turning back."

"Then said Jesus unto the twelve, 'Will ye also go away?' Then Simon Peter answered him, 'Lord, to whom shall we go? You have the words of eternal life. And we believe and are sure that You are the Messiah, the Son of the living God'." John 6:67-69

## 12-10
### Fear And Love

People who are prone to fear will not only find it in the shadows; they will find it in full light. Fear is a terrible way to live our lives. We can draw up long lists of people whom we should fear. The Holy Scriptures always direct us away from fear. It is said that there are 365 "Do-not-fears" in the Bible, one for every day of the year. God's love for us generates in us a love for God where fear of God is taken away. Abba loves all people, even the ones we think we should fear. His kind of love in us causes us to move toward all people and all people groups instead of running away in fear. We need this God's-kind-of-love to transform us and them. With it we can live with our neighbors without fear.

"Such love has no fear, because perfect love expels all fear. If we are afraid, it is for fear of punishment, and this shows that we have not fully experienced his perfect love. We love each other because he loved us first." 1 John 4:18-19 (NLT)

## 12-11
### Fully Experiencing God (1)

We have not yet gotten hold of a simple but profound truth in Scripture. It is this: THE WAY WE RELATE TO PEOPLE SHOWS THAT WE HAVE, OR HAVE NOT, EXPERIENCED GOD THE WAY HE IS. Read this carefully: "Such love has no fear, because perfect love expels all fear. If we are afraid, it is for fear of punishment, and THIS SHOWS THAT WE HAVE NOT FULLY EXPERIENCED HIS PERFECT LOVE" (1 John 4:18B NLT). Soak that in for a minute! We experience God's love as mercy and grace. If we are not living our lives in unconditional love, generous mercy and grace, then we have not come to know God like God is. To experience God as He truly is keeps on transforming our actions and all human relationships. Living out the true knowledge of our Abba is forever bringing us to maturity.

## 12-12
### Fully Experiencing God (2)
God does not engineer the events of our lives, but He does, through the events of our lives, engineer us by His Spirit. Because He is love, He allows us to choose. Our choices and the collective choices of other humans, past and present, have created the circumstances and events of our lives. God does not sit aloof from what is going on in the stream of our lives and human history, but has entered it through incarnation. It is His goal to shape us like our Lord Jesus through everything that is happening to us. Running away in actuality or imagination only postpones what He is wanting to reveal of Himself at the moment. When we learn to act and react in a Christlike manner, we experience the God who is; He inhabits Christlike actions and reactions.

"And we know that God causes everything to work together for the good of those who love God and are called according to his purpose for them. For God knew his people in advance, and he chose them to become like his Son, so that his Son would be the firstborn among many brothers and sisters." Romans 8:28-29 (NLT)

## 12-13
### Atonement And The Spirit
Nothing skews our understanding of God's reconciling atoning work like leaving the Holy Spirit out of the atonement equation. Atonement is the totality of who Christ is and what He has set in motion. It is the incarnation, Calvary, resurrection, Pentecost, ascension, intercession and more. There are many atonement theories, none of which can stand alone, but only in tension with each other and never without the Spirit. Simply because, we can never be at-one-ment with God without the Spirit of the Christ living inside of us. Jesus called the Spirit, "I in them" (John 17:23). The root idea of atonement is unity with God. The washing of regeneration makes possible the abiding Spirit who unites us to our Father. Hallelujah!

## 12-14
### Entertainment vs. Worship
Worship can degenerate into entertainment. Entertainment is about the people as the audience. Worship is about God being the audience. One is "me" centered and the other is "God" centered. Blessed is the congregation whose worship is centered in God. We add lights, sounds and props so we can create mood and atmosphere that compete with the entertainment industry. The Spirit of God is not a mood; He creates His own Atmosphere! Quiet your heart. Listen to His word being read! Be silent before Him! Center in Him! Bow before Him! Praise Him! This kind of worship is light years ahead of entertainment.

Father, we are Your congregants gathered around You for worship. Forgive us when we center in other things and not You. May we examine our own hearts so that we are worshiping You in Spirit and truth. Amen.

## 12-15
### Works And Righteousness
The evangelical church's fear of "works' righteousness" has enabled us to throw the baby out with the bath water. Of course we do not believe that we can earn our salvation by the works we do, but what we overlook is that to live righteously involves works. Righteousness is the process of living out what is just and right. It is the way we live our life in this world. It is doing good deeds for the bodies and souls of human kind in all the places and ways we have opportunity.

"He gave his life to free us from every kind of sin, to cleanse us, and to make us his very own people, totally committed to doing good deeds." Titus 2:14 (NLT)

## 12-16
### Earth Mirrors Heaven
The ancient tabernacle was built after a heavenly pattern (Hebrews 8:5). Our worship on earth is to reflect and be in harmony with the worship that is now occurring in heaven (Revelation 4-5); we are to join the songs the angels in heaven sing. We are to pray that the will of God be done on earth as it is done in heaven; we are to mirror heaven at doing the will of God (The Lord's Prayer). Earthly marriages are to reflect the heavenly marriage that Christ has with His church (Ephesians 5:32). We are to live out the image of our heavenly Father as

His image-bearers in the world. How are we doing at reflecting God's great glory in this dark world?

## 12-17
### Pursuing Truth
We are people pursuing truth. We pursue truth not as though we have not found it, but we pursue truth to follow it to the conclusions to which it leads us. Truth matters. All truth, including scientific, is derived from God. We need not fear any truth, from simple scientific truth to complex quantum physics, from simple doctrine to profound theology; it is God's truth. The church neglects doctrine to its own demise. The creeds were meant to teach. In the ideal congregation the pastor is a resident theologian educating believers in the grand and existing truths of Christianity. When ignorance is exalted and truth is neglected, empty phrases, half-truths and heresies will fill the void. Worship services should educate by being saturated with Scripture reading and preaching that carefully and accurately expounds biblical truth.

"He will not stop until the earth is as full of the knowledge of the LORD as the waters cover the sea" (Isa 11:9).

## 12-18
### Our Example For Humility
How do you humble yourself to get below: the Babe born in a cattle stall and laid in a manger, the One who became poor to enrich you with grace, the King who rides a donkey, the Messiah who washes feet, the Master who became a slave for you, the One who was God and became human, the One who died on a cross for you, and the One Who by His own death defeated your death? This model of the humility of our Lord should create genuine humility in us.

"Have this attitude in yourselves which was also in Christ Jesus, who, although He existed in the form of God, did not regard equality with God a thing to be grasped, but emptied Himself, taking the form of a bond-servant, and being made in the likeness of men. Being found in appearance as a man, He humbled Himself by becoming obedient to the point of death, even death on a cross." Philippians 2:5-8 (NASB)

**12-19**
**Love Is Of One Piece**
Jesus taught that the greatest commandment is to love God with your whole heart, soul and mind; the extension of that is to love your neighbor as yourself (Matthew 22:35-40). The apostle John said that love for God is not present if we did not love our brothers and sisters. Love dwells in our lives as a whole piece; to divide love for God and neighbor is to distort and destroy it. To hold ourselves, our neighbor and our God in a circle of flowing love is the vision the Father has for all peoples of the earth. It is the mark of all who have been born of God (1 John 4:7).

"Those who do not love a brother or sister whom they have seen, cannot love God whom they have not seen. The commandment we have from him is this: those who love God must love their brothers and sisters also." 1 John 4:20b-21 (NRSV)

**12-20**
**A Broken World**
We live in a broken world; we too are broken. It descends through our DNA and resonates in our cells. We live our lives from our own brokenness and the brokenness of all those around us. Because we are broken we sometimes love the wrong things, being drawn to things that can lead to further brokenness. We are in need of healing. To admit our brokenness is the path to our healing. To be patient with our broken neighbors is righteousness and can become their rescue and way forward; this looks like the Kingdom of God.

**12-21**
**The Power Of The Cross**
The cross was a symbol that someone else had the power, even power to put Jesus to death. It looked like the empire had triumphed with the last word. "King of the Jews", in mockery, was put over the cross. But the one with the real power was not Caesar, Herod, nor Pilate. Messiah demonstrated His power, not by military might, not by returning evil for evil, nor death for death, and without vengeance, retaliation and retribution He showed the kind of power that the weak can never show. He showed the radical power of unconditional love, unearned mercy, and complete forgiveness. There is no power in the universe which can match that.

**12-22**
**Be A Jesus' Follower**
Some folks want Jesus to hand them a ticket to heaven without any intention of following Him. They would like to use Him without a real surrender of their lives to Him. Following Jesus' teaching as a way of being in the world is considered unnecessary, so long as we have our ticket, but Jesus says, "If anyone serves Me, he must follow Me" (John 12:26a). To be a Christian should mean, above all other things, that we are followers of the lowly Nazarene.

"If anyone wishes to come after Me, he must deny himself, and take up his cross daily and follow Me. 'For whoever wishes to save his life will lose it, but whoever loses his life for My sake, he is the one who will save it." Luke 9:23-24 (NASB)

**12-23**
**The Creator Came Down**
He who made the world showed up in the world. He who was one with the Father became one with us. He came to where we are to take us where He is; that is, He became what we are so that we could become what He is, sons and daughters of God. He entered into us so that we could enter into Him. No one could redeem us, except the One who made us. It is in receiving Him that we embrace the Creator as our Redeemer; it is in receiving the divine Grace-Energy of the Cosmic-Christ-Creator-Redeemer that we are born children of God. Hallelujah, what a Savior!

"He was in the world, and the world was made through him, yet the world did not know him. He came to his own, and his own people did not receive him. But to all who did receive him, who believed in his name, he gave the right to become children of God, who were born, not of blood nor of the will of the flesh nor of the will of man, but of God." John 1:10-13 (ESV)

**12-24**
**No Room**
No room in the inn (Luke 2:7) was always a sad moment to me in a Christmas play. Still, we are too busy; our lives are so full that we cannot find room for the Christ. There is no room in our daily schedules nor our week, no room in our priorities, and no room in our thoughts. What we love is always that for which we

will make room. It is about what we love; it is about what really matters in our lives. Love Him enough to give Him, not just a room, but the whole house.

The persons who "do not seek God" and "in all his thoughts" has "no room for God" are called wicked (Psalm 10:4 NIV).

## 12-25
### Jesus Is
Friend. Brother. Son. Master. Priest. Sacrifice. Redeemer. Justifier. Sanctifier. Hope. Human. Divine. Teacher. Healer. Physician. Mystery. Bread. Water. Wine. Vine. Path. Way. Road. Shepherd. Faithful. Witness. Wisdom. Righteousness. Prophet. Word. Lion. Lamb. Light. Intercessor. Advocate. Counselor. Messiah. Savior. Lord. King.

"For to us a child is born, to us a son is given, and the government will be on his shoulders. And he will be called Wonderful Counselor, Mighty God, Everlasting Father, Prince of Peace. Of the increase of his government and peace there will be no end. He will reign on David's throne and over his kingdom, establishing and upholding it with justice and righteousness from that time on and forever. The zeal of the LORD Almighty will accomplish this." Isaiah 9:6-7 (NIV)

## 12-26
### Out of Egypt
"When Israel was a child, I loved him, and out of Egypt I called my son" (Hosea 11:1 ESV). Israel coming out of Egypt was the first Passover: the great salvation rescue, the great redemption. Jesus was the second Passover. He Himself is the sacrificial Lamb whose blood sprinkled over the doorpost of our lives ends what the death angel can do. He also came to bring us out of sin's captivity, giving us freedom; He came to become our Promised Land.

"So Joseph got up and took the Child and His mother while it was still night, and left for Egypt. He remained there until the death of Herod. This was to fulfill what had been spoken by the Lord through the prophet: "OUT OF EGYPT I CALLED MY SON." Matthew 2:14-15 (NASB)

## 12-27
### Christmas Tears
The wise men searching for a future Jewish king disturbed Herod to his core. What followed was the slaughter of Bethlehem's male children, age two and under; children unjustly killed by a power-hungry insecure king. The tears and sorrow of mothers and fathers that sad night is a forgotten part of Christmas story. Tears, sorrow, depression and grief still visit during the Christmas season. Sad memories, past hurts, present dysfunction, loneliness, poverty, random evil may all bring Christmas tears. Let's be sensitive in our joys to those who are experiencing sorrow.

"A voice was heard in Ramah, wailing and loud lamentation, Rachel weeping for her children; she refused to be consoled, because they are no more." Matthew 2:18 (NRSV)

## 12-28
### The Universal Invitation
The Jewish shepherds came to Messiah first; two years later Gentile Magi came. The gospel went out first to the Jews and then to all the world. The gospel is the good news that the promised Messiah of the Jews is, in fact, Lord of the whole earth, which includes Gentiles. There are to be no strangers, foreigners and aliens who are not included. All are invited to eat bread in the Kingdom of God. The holy universal (catholic) church is rooted in the universal invitation. We who received such a generous invitation must extend it with the same generosity.

"And the Spirit and the bride say, Come. And let him that hears say, Come. And let him that is thirsty come. And whosoever will, let him take the water of life freely." Revelation 22:17

## 12-29
### The Grand Invitation
Hear this grand invitation, "Come to me" and "Take my yoke"; this is the solution to so much of what troubles and burdens us. I have to keep going to Him with my pain. I have to readjust and take up the yoke again and again. My old patterns of coping don't serve me well. His yoke gets me through a lot of hurt and disappointment. Fretting and worry do not work; anxiety and fear are just

further downers. Lord, I come to You for soul rest and I take Your yoke for labor and living.

"Come to me, all who labor and are heavy laden, and I will give you rest. Take my yoke upon you, and learn from me, for I am gentle and lowly in heart, and you will find rest for your souls. For my yoke is easy, and my burden is light."
Matthew 11:28-30 (ESV)

## 12-30
### Incarnation

The incarnation is far more than a miracle conception. It reaffirms God's original word that creation is good. Matter is not evil. The human body is not evil. In Jesus, the divine and human met in undivided wholeness. He was not half human and half God; He was fully human and fully God. Jesus, by the indwelling Spirit makes us children of God. This brings us not only into the family of God, but into the mission of God. We are born from above to bring heavenly life down to earth as Jesus did.

"But to all who did receive him, who believed in his name, he gave the right to become children of God, who were born, not of blood nor of the will of the flesh nor of the will of man, but of God. And the Word became flesh and dwelt among us, and we have seen his glory, glory as of the only Son from the Father, full of grace and truth… For from his fullness we have all received, grace upon grace."
John 1:12-14,16 (ESV)

## 12-31
### The Year That is Past

This past year had in it both the bad and the good, both the sorrowful and the happy. I still see shortcomings and failures in my own personality that make me sad, and which I confess to my Lord. I also see good things that He accomplished in me and through me. I do not believe that we are saved by the good in our life outweighing the bad. We are saved by grace, pure and simple, unearned and generous. The Lord of Grace will walk with me into my future with His un-diminishing love; it never wanes and it never fails. I am at peace with that; I embrace His astonishing grace.

**Benediction**
Now to the King eternal, immortal, invisible, the only God, be honor and glory forever and ever. Amen." 1 Timothy 1:17 (NASB)

## Other Books by H. Lamar Smith

In Paperback and Kindle

### In The Steps of The Shepherd
*366 Short Thoughts for the Long Walk*

### The Disciples and The Teacher
*366 Short Thoughts for Serious Disciples*

### Staying On The Way
*366 Short Thoughts for 'Walking The Jesus' Way*

### Springs In Dry Places
*366 Short Thoughts For Thirsty Souls*

### Captives Of Love
*366 Short Thoughts For Christ's Bond Servants*

### The Master's Table
366 Short Thoughts For Hungry Disciples

Made in the USA
Lexington, KY
17 December 2019